HEART & HABITS

How We Change For Good

Greg E. Gifford

Unless otherwise indicated, all Scripture quotations are from The 2011 English Standard Version, Wheaton, IL, Crossway Publication.

Published by:

www.kressbiblical.com

ISBN: 978-1-934952-57-3

HEART
&
HABITS

DEDICATION

To Amber: You are the butter to my bread, the breath to my life.
Your love moves me and makes me better.

To Zane and Finn: I'm so thankful to be your Dad.
Follow me as I follow Christ.

To Faith Community Church: You are my family, my friends,
and my community. I love you.
Thanks for letting me be one of your pastors!

To the Students at The Master's University: You are the best
and brightest and I'm truly not worthy to be your professor.
I want to spend my one, short life serving you.

CONTENTS

CHAPTER 1

FAN THE FLAME THROUGH FREQUENT PRACTICE

If you haven't built a fire by this point in your life, you're missing out! When I was growing up, my family enjoyed camping in the Appalachian foothills of Northern Georgia and the Carolinas. When it was time for the sun to go down, sitting around the fire was just about all there was to do on the lazy camping night. We'd get everything ready for the fire and typically attempt to start the fire as the sun was going down or dinner time—whichever came first. The process of building a fire isn't complicated, but it isn't easy either: go gather some wood, find something that would serve as a kindling, and grab your lighter. It's not complicated, but it does take work. We would prepare for our fire by gathering wood for the fire during the day, so when nighttime came, we would already have enough firewood. Nobody likes searching for firewood in the dark!

When starting the fire, you place the kindling in the firepit and get a small flame going. The small flame catches a log or two on fire, and then you have yourself a fire! Yet, as the evening progresses, the fire begins to die out and you have to rally to find some wood, place it in the fire, and stoke the fire. To maintain the fire does take work, to be sure; it takes the work of gathering wood and adding it to the fire. But once the spark of the first fire begins, it is much easier to maintain.

Habit development is much like building a fire. In habit development, you need to go collect the wood by developing good habits. For some, this is easier, like simply picking up pieces, while for others, there is heavy-duty log lifting that lies ahead, perhaps even some wood splitting. Bring an axe with you! You need to have the wood ready to throw into the fire, if and when you get that initial spark of change in your life. You will need to stoke the change with good habits, otherwise the change will begin to die out. Despite our efforts in habit development, all the work of gathering the firewood is contingent on the spark of that first flame. The Puritans would say that only God can bring that first spark of change.

In the 1600s, there was a group of theologians who were astute in their ability to apply the complexities of the Bible to daily life—these theologians are known as the English Puritans. They were theologians who remained in the church of England and wanted to see reform take place in the church—thus they were "Puritans" as opposed to "Separatists." One English Puritan, Thomas Watson, said of our habits in the spiritual sphere of our lives, "What I have spoken is to encourage faith, not indulge sloth. Do not think God will do our work for us while we sit still. As God will blow up the spark of grace by His Spirit, so we must be blowing it up by holy efforts."[1]

We could lie down next to the fire pit and pray that God would send a lightning bolt to start the fire and sustain it, but building a fire doesn't typically work like that, and neither do habits. Making no effort in our habits and saying, "Please Lord, bring about change in our lives!" is like saying "Please Lord, cause a flame by a lightning strike" while we lie in a comatose state next to the fire pit. That's not the way fires get started and it's not the way God will bring change.

Your habits are much like the fire: you have a responsibility to work and gather—to chop, to harvest, to stoke—but once you've started the habit, like the fire, things get much easier. When the fire is already burning, it's really more about maintenance. Yes, it still takes work to sustain the habit, but the habit itself is already helping and making it easier. Although habits make things easier, our habits never determine who we will be or the directions our lives *must* go. It's through the freeing power of God's grace, and his Spirit,

---

1   Thomas Watson, *The Godly Man's Picture* (Carlisle, PA: Banner of Truth, 1666), 237.

that we are no longer slaves to habits of sin and self-destruction. But our habits do make it easier to sustain change in our lives—or easier to extinguish change.

However, Watson made a great point: only God can cause the initial spark of change. No matter how much work you do, only God can bring about genuine change in your life. Despite all the habits that you attempt to develop, if God doesn't bring that initial spark, then there is no fire. You can chop and gather all

No matter how much work you do, only God can bring about genuine change in your life.

you want, but there will still be no fire. God blows up the spark by his Spirit; we blow up the spark by our efforts. That balance of God's work and our work is essential to understanding habit development.

Campfires also have purposes for their creation: to warm the food, warm the body, cook some S'mores, burn stuff, or just enjoy watching the dancing flames. Whatever they are, you create a fire with one or more of those purposes in mind. Likewise, you are creating habits with purposes in mind, too. Sometimes we think of efficiency and productivity or an area of personal change as the ultimate purpose. In this book, however, I hope to show you that God uses habits to accomplish his purposes in your life. You may have picked up this book with personal goals already, and I don't want to cast overboard any purpose that you already possess. But I do want to show you how to use those habits for the glory of God and the good of other people first, then to accomplish your secondary goals.

THE PURPOSES OF HABITS
The Glory of God

Sometimes when we say, "the glory of God," it's a bit like white noise: we've heard the term so much that we shrug it off in agreement. But the glory of God is the *primary* reason for our habits. When I say, "glory of God," I want you to think of valuing and pleasing God. When we value something, we honor, prize, adore, praise, cherish, and admire that thing. When we value

God, we honor him, prize him, adore him, praise him, cherish him, and admire him. Think of glory as weight on a scale. God is weightier and more to be prized than any other thing.

When we please God, we live our lives in a way that God likes, according to his Word. This provides massive significance to our habits because our habits can actually please God! Paul says in 2 Corinthians 5:9 that "whether we are home or away, we make it our aim to please him." You can please God habitually. And when we glorify God, we please him. When we please God, we glorify him. Don't let the familiarity of the phrase "glory of God" become white noise, and I will try not to be a noisemaker in this book. However, I will repeatedly prompt you to remember that the main purpose of our habits is for the glory, valuing, and pleasure of God!

...the main purpose of our habits is for the glory, valuing, and pleasure of God!

The Good of People

The secondary goal of habits is that people would be blessed by our habits. The Bible makes it clear that we are to love God supremely and then to love our neighbors in the same way we love ourselves (Matt. 22:37-38). Your habits are simply a part of this equation. Your habits can and should be a means of you doing good to those who are around you. You want others to be blessed, helped, encouraged, edified, strengthened, equipped, or loved by the things that you habitually do.

Your habits also are for your highest good. The good of people includes, well, you. As you habitually communicate in a godly way, as you habitually resolve conflict in a godly way, then you will be blessed by those habits. But this is the biblical order—others, then you. Philippians 2:5 makes it clear that Jesus had the mind to serve others before himself. And in the verse before, Paul says, "Let each of you look not only to his own interests, but also to the interests of others" (Phil. 2:4). Habits aren't about you first, but habits do bless you. And habits do benefit you. They are "in our interest," we could say. Later in this book, I'll discuss more about the "good for you" components of habits.

THE EFFECTS OF HABITS

The purpose of habits segues into the effects of habits, which is where most books on habits focus, and also where readers tend to focus. We want to know how to get results, how to accomplish goals, how to improve relationships, and so forth. Those are effects of habits. Habits have three-overarching effects: (1) shaping your desires, (2) shaping your character, and (3) helping with daily functioning.

What if you were so accustomed to obeying God that you now obeyed him out of habit? For instance, think of people who are good listeners. They no longer need to say to themselves, "Wait for this person to be done speaking"—they simply wait for the other person to be done speaking. They've practiced kindness so much that they no longer talk over people or interrupt them while they're speaking. Kindness in speech has now become habitual for them. Or what if you were so accustomed to thinking God's thoughts after him that you immediately think of his protecting power right after a car accident, even before you think about getting the other person's insurance information? You've made a habit of meditating on the Bible and now, in a moment of crisis, you are thinking about your car accident the way God thinks about your car accident. Sounds good, right? Well, those are examples of the effects of habits.

Desires Are Oriented Through Habits

Philosophers have repeatedly said, "You do what you want," because at the core of each of our decisions, we are driven by desires. Sometimes those desires are murky or conflicted, but they are desires nevertheless. But did you know that what you do shapes what you want to do? The Bible speaks of how our regular practices shape our desires. One example of this is the habit of gathering with your local church. The author of Hebrews says that some neglect this gathering out of habit (Heb. 10:25). Gathering with your local church is a habit that shapes your desires!

...did you know that what you do shapes what you want to do?

This principle is one of the most significant ideas to grasp in habit development. Many of us are plagued with a lack of desire in areas where we know we need to change. Yet, that lack of desire isn't going to change until we begin to change our habits. It's through God's help that we change our habits, and that results in a change of what we want.

Character Is Formed Through Habits

A classical way to understand the effects of habits is to speak of *habitus*, or character. Aristotle said, "You are what you repeatedly do." Character formation comes through practice. Unlike desire formation, character formation is about the type of person you are. Whereas desire formation is the type of person you want to become, character formation is who you actually become. You are a loving person by practicing love. You are a wise person by practicing wisdom. You are a gentle person by practicing gentleness. Habits form or de-form character in you. The author of Hebrews says that the mature in the faith have their "powers of discernment trained by constant practice to distinguish good from evil" (Heb. 5:14).

This effect of habits is one that you as parent and grandparent are intimately familiar with as you seek to help children form certain types of character. Whether it's sharing a toy, or working on table manners, parents and grandparents are helping their children form character through frequent practice. Other times, character is formed through the habit of serving others. For example, after our kids moved out of the house, my wife and I began to serve others in our local church more and more. It's that habit of serving others that helps us to be considerate and giving. That's because habits form character. If there are pockets of undeveloped character in our lives, then there needs to be an analysis of undeveloped habits, because the one affects the other.

Lost Without Them in Daily Functioning

Have you ever paused to think about all that our habits do for us on a daily basis? We are basically at the mercy of our daily habits. Consider the following activities for a moment: (1) walking, (2) driving a car, and (3) reading.

Perhaps it's been a while, but most of us learned the habit of walking at a very young age. I still have young kids at home, and it hasn't been too long since I helped my children learn how to walk. It starts with that first footstep on their own, then progresses from the coffee table to the couch with some assistance. Finally, regular practice produces a total agility where our children are free and we have to chase them everywhere. In this process, my kids are learning habits—habits that we adults have somewhat mastered. And how did we learn to perform such complex feats? It was through the repeated, frequent practice of placing one foot in front of the other over a long time. To be honest, we don't think a whole lot about the level of muscular coordination that it takes to walk these days—we simply walk.

Consider another example: driving. It's interesting because driving is also a habit that has been learned over years of practice. Like walking, none of us were born with the ability to drive (that means you, too, NASCAR fans!) but rather all of us *learned* how to drive. At this point, though, driving is so hardwired into us that you can plop us in a rental car that we have never driven before and we can adjust the seat, shift the transmission into drive, and accelerate with very little thought or effort. Moreover, we can change lanes with the corresponding blinker, knowing instinctively that up is right and down is left—not to mention many of us can do all this in a manual-transmission vehicle, too. We can do this because of the power of habit. Could you imagine if every time we drove our car, we had to think consciously to ourselves, *Press the brake. Now shift into drive. Release the brake. Now accelerate the vehicle. Turn the steering wheel toward the direction you want to go,* and so forth? Yikes! If you think some of us drive slowly now, imagine if you removed our habits!

One final example of the indispensability of habit is the skill of read-

...right now you are practicing an amazing skill attained through habit.

ing. Like with walking and driving, reading is a habit that you develop. You might not have considered this, but right now you are practicing an amazing skill attained through habit. Most of you have associated meaning with words and memorized those words so that you don't have to phonetically pronounce each word. Pho-ne-tic-all-ly pro-noun-cing e-ach wo-rd. Get it? You see the word and associate it with a meaning that you have formerly committed to memory. Thus, your "level of reading" isn't normally your ability to phonetically pronounce words. No, rather, it's how quickly you can see the word, associate meaning to it, and comprehend it in light of the overall paragraph. And that all comes from habit. Most of us have seen the word "the" so many times that we don't use phonetics at all; we just know it's "the."

Our habits are such a pervasive part of our lives that we'd be lost without them. Some have estimated that our habits comprise at least 71% of all that we do on a daily basis—that's incredible! So, if we didn't have the power of habit, we'd have to intentionally and deliberately think about each step in processes like walking, driving, and reading. It's really quite phenomenal and scary all at once! You would never be able to finish reading this book, or even walk across the room to pick it up, if it weren't for habits!

HABITS ARE PERVASIVE, YET NOT DETERMINATIVE

However, a Christian understanding of habits is that we control them—they don't control us. Our habits can make it easier to do good or evil, but we always still have the choice since our habits never determine who we will be. The Bible teaches that we have control over our actions, and this includes control over our habits. At no point have we lost the ability to break unhelpful or even sinful habits, because we have God's resources for this change.

The Bible says that Christians are never in a position where they *must* sin (1 Cor. 10:13; Rom. 6:19)—habitually or otherwise. God has freed his children from the power of sin and the bondage of sin through Jesus. Amen! And we are also not slaves to unhelpful habits that are not necessarily sinful. Through awareness, knowledge of the habit, specific steps to grow, and God's help, every Christian can form more helpful, God-honoring habits. We can always change, which is incredibly hopeful news!

Therefore, when we say that our habits are pervasive, we mean that. And when we say that we are not controlled by our habits, we mean that also. The Bible calls us to not be controlled by anything except the Holy Spirit in our lives (Eph. 5:18). He alone gets to sit in the driver's seat. Yet, there is a sense in which we can recognize these truths and still find that our habits can be "on autopilot" in the sense that you haven't even paused to think about them. An illustration of this is when you catch yourself chewing with your mouth wide open. Other unknown habits are like chewing food with your mouth wide open: you may have a choice to close your mouth, but you have to learn it's open to begin with! Many times, we simply haven't paused long enough to consider the unknown habits that are on autopilot—*but they still don't control us.*

UNKNOWN HABITS

The Bible teaches that none of us are slaves to our habits, but am I saying that some of us have habits we are unaware of? Well, yes, that's exactly what I am saying. While it's important to maintain human responsibility, it is also important to say that certain people have developed habits unbeknownst to themselves (like checking social media instead of finishing that email, without even thinking about it). I see it in the counseling context when couples have habits of communication that hurt a relationship. Or, when habits of time management slowly dry up relationships because we've dedicated every waking minute to work. Sometimes my counselees wonder, "How did this happen?" And I can unequivocally say that they have developed habits unbeknownst to themselves.

We often need more knowledge to expose the unknown habits that we've developed. We'll talk about this more in a later chapter, but that knowledge can come from many sources—anything from self-realization to an outside problem that arises. Maybe we've grown in self-awareness unintentionally, like when we happen to see a picture of ourselves and think, "Wow, I really need to lose some weight!" Other times, knowledge of an unknown habit can come through a problem. The dentist tells us that we need to floss more, or the doctor tells us that we need to work on our cholesterol. We've fallen into these habits and haven't realized it until a problem develops. When confronted with such a problem and its causes, we think, *Oh yeah, I do that, don't I?*

Naturally, I help people discover these unknown habits in my line of work as counselor. That illustrates how a third party can often be brought into our lives to help us gain perspective on blind spots. How are we not thinking according to God's Word? What is it that we are doing that we're not aware of? Is there something that's simply unhelpful in our lives?

Whatever the means, which we will discuss thoroughly in this book, identifying unknown habits always comes through growing in knowledge. Simply put, we seldom change if we don't know what needs to be changed.

Unknown habits are probably the most lethal types of habits because we aren't aware of them. And, again, don't think that I'm necessarily speaking of

...we seldom change if we don't know what needs to be changed.

things that are direct, willful steps away from God's will. No, rather, this could look like a family that has fallen into the habit of watching TV while they eat dinner together. Instead of turning the TV off and eating at the table, they spend that 45 minutes in front of the TV. That unknown habit can take a serious, long-term toll on their family. And the scary part is that they weren't even aware that they were doing that. Worse yet are the unknown habits that are clearly against God's will for our lives. It's hard to comprehend that we not only do things that God doesn't like, but we can do them habitually without awareness. This book will help you identify and change unknown habits.

HABITS AND BEHAVIORISM

If something is broken, then just fix it, right? Is it that easy? This is where we want to be really cautious because we don't want to come across as auto mechanics in our approach to habits: "Well, if you simply replace this habit with that habit, then your life will run properly. That'll be $450." That's way too reductionistic and is part of what has prevented us as Christians from talking helpfully about habits up to this point.

John B. Watson, an early-twentieth-century psychologist, coined the term "behaviorism" and was a self-proclaimed "behaviorist." Essentially, a behavioristic approach is when a person thinks that they simply need to tweak his behavior and replace it with a more desirable behavior and *voila*, all is well. Yet, we recognize that people are not the sum total of their behaviors. In fact, the Bible spends much time talking about the immaterial heart, soul, spirit, and mind—the inner person. Listen to the words of Proverbs 4:23: "Keep your heart with all vigilance, from it flow the springs of life." We cannot merely become auto-mechanic habit-fixers, because then we've missed the very reason why we develop habits in the first place, which is because of the heart.

Behavior Modification as a *Dangerous* Necessity

J.B. Watson rightly terrifies us by minimizing the importance of the heart in changing behavior. To speak of only changing behavior is dangerous because it shifts focus from the *why* of your actions to the *what* of your actions. The Bible consistently says that there is not only a call for the "what" but also a call for the "why"—for both the doing and the desiring. For example, Jesus condemned the Pharisees and Scribes with the same accusations that were levied against the children of Israel: "This people honors me with their lips, but their heart is far from me" (Matt. 15:8; Isa. 29:13). Be careful about changing only your behavior!

But behavior modification is still necessary. The Bible tells us to avoid certain behaviors: don't lie, don't steal, don't use corrupt speech, etc. We are called to modify our behavior out of right motivations from the heart. We find ourselves living in the tension of our hearts not fully desiring God's will for our life and the call to do what God wants us to do whether we immediately want it or not. Think of two paths that converge upon each other: one path being God's will and one being our will. The development of habits brings about the convergence of our will to God's will through Spirit-filled obedience. Behavior modification through habit formation is essential to our Christian walk—developing the behaviors that God expects of us while authentically desiring to please him from our hearts. Only the Holy Spirit can transform your heart, but your behavior modifications are necessary and often used as kindling for the fire of your spiritual maturity. John Owen described good habits as simply moral habits: "Moral habits are nothing but strong and firm dispositions and inclinations unto moral acts and duties of their own kind; as righteousness, or temperance, or meekness."[2] A person should have moral habits even before they became a Christian. You say "thank you" or open the door for the person behind you. Perhaps you allow a person to enter your lane when driving? Those are all habits that are necessary and right.

There is a moral good to good habits that comes through behavior modification, though it still may lack the redemptive good that can only come through Jesus' death for us. So, don't reject behavior modification; reject behavior modification that is void of any discussion of the need for a transformed heart. Teach your grandchildren to say "please" and "thank you," but teach them that we practice those habits out of a heart that wants to please God. Anything else will result in a crippling despair when we fail or a rank self-righteousness when we succeed.

HEART AND HABITS

This book will emphasize the role of the heart in habit development. It's the immaterial heart of man that explains why we do the things that we do: both for good reasons (Matt. 22:37) and also for not-so-good reasons (Mark 7:21-23). A book on habits must talk about the heart—that's why the title is *Heart & Habits*. Emphasizing the heart is what balances a *distinctively* Christian book on habits because it's not about external habits only—it's about our motivations to develop habits in the first place. That's the heart. That's what keeps us from being behavioristic.

But we can be imbalanced the other way, as well. A fear of behaviorism has kept good Christian authors from developing resources on habits. The conversation about habits has largely been relegated to savvy businesspeople, marketing teams, and sociologists. Whatever the reason, there hasn't been

2   John Owen, *The Works of John Owen*, Vol. 3 (Carlisle, PA: Banner of Truth, 1965), 3:18-19.

a significant conversation about habits from a biblical perspective by Christian authors since the English Puritans—and they wrote in the 1600s![3]

...there hasn't been a significant conversation about habits from a biblical perspective by Christian authors since the English Puritans...

WHAT TO EXPECT FROM THIS BOOK

The over-arching purpose of this book is to help you understand the heart as it informs your habits, so you can develop habits for the glory of God and the good of people. Like a river, your habits have a source, and that's your heart. And like the currents in a river, habits propel you, facilitate movement, and incline you toward certain ends, but your heart is the source of what you do—including your habits. So, unlike other books on habit, this one will contain a lot of discussion about the inner person that leads us toward habit development. If a book on habits misses the heart, it may just miss the whole point.

---

3   In the modern era, Christians who want to study habit development have had to read mostly secular works like those of William James, Charles Duhigg's *The Power of Habit*, BJ Fogg's theory of "tiny habits," or James Clear's *Atomic Habits*. The best resource we have by a Christian is James K.A. Smith's work, *Desiring the Kingdom*, but Smith approaches habits from a philosophical standpoint.

CHAPTER 2

WHAT ARE HABITS? AND WHY DO THEY MAKE "ALL THE DIFFERENCE"?

In his book *Nicomachean Ethics*, Aristotle writes, "It makes no small difference, then, whether we form habits of one kind or of another from our very youth; it makes a very great difference, or rather all the difference." There's a sense in which it's hard to overstate the importance of habit formation. Some have described habits as being like a pathway, and that with each step down the pathway, there is an increasing familiarity that is hard to undo. Furthermore, there is now an inclination to follow that same pathway the next time we walk that direction. If habits do comprise 71% of our daily activities, as I previously suggested, it's apparent that the way that we think about habits is extremely important. So, first of all, let's pause and talk through a few key terms to describe exactly what habits are and then what makes them so important. To begin, then, we must identify our terms. When we speak of habit, we are speaking of *regular, frequent practices that seem almost second nature.*

DEFINITION OF HABIT

That definition of habit summarizes what some important historical sources have said about the issue, and most importantly what the Bible says.

Habit (as Action)

To speak of a habit as regular, frequent practice is to speak of what would also be known as a "natural habit" by the English Puritans.[4] When you think of a natural habit, think of the things that you can learn to do with automaticity[5]—things like driving, reading, walking, saying "please" and "thank you," and cleaning up after yourself. Those are natural habits in the sense that any person can develop them through regular practice. When discussing natural habits, some have treated them as reflexes. Russian physiologist Ivan Pavlov would use this understanding of habits to create his theory of conditioning.[6] William James, the father of American psychology, said that habits are the result of "nerve-currents" in the brain traveling the same path repeatedly.[7] Both of these men placed a high emphasis on the physiological components of habits. They would, perhaps unwittingly, affirm the idea of habits as regular, frequent practices. "What fires together, wires together," they might say.

Habit (as Virtue)

Yet there is another historical way to speak of habits. Aristotle is famous for many reasons, one of which is speaking to the ideas of ethics and virtue. It

---

4   James Nichols, *Puritan Sermons, 1659-1689*, vol. 1–5 (Wheaton, IL: R.O. Roberts, 1981), 4:273.

5   Routines are similar to habits in that a routine is a series of various practice and a habit is a reference to one, singular practice repeated. Some, like James Clear, have used the idea of 'compounding habits', which would typically refer to a routine or series of habits (cf. James Clear, *Atomic Habits: An Easy & Proven Way to Build Good Habits & Break Bad Ones* (New York, NY: Avery, 2018). We could say that you have a nighttime routine of brushing your teeth, putting on pajamas, and plugging in your phone to charge. Those are individual habits that comprise a routine.

6   Ivan Pavlov, *Lectures on Conditioned Reflexes* (New York, NY: New York International Publishers, 1928), 296-97.

7   William James, *Writings, 1878-1899* (New York, NY: The Library of America, 1992), 137.

was Aristotle's virtue that would also be spoken of as a habit, also known as *habitus*. In Aristotle's writing, habit and virtue were often used interchangeably. When discussing the issue, he spoke of habit as including the ideas of character and nature.[8] (Think less of practices that you frequently perform and more of the broad characterizations of who you are.) Where we would tend to use the term "character," Aristotle would refer to *virtue*. If we said, "He is a kind person," Aristotle would see that kindness as a virtue. In this sense, we could rightly say, "You have habits because of habits." This means you have regular practices of kindness that seem second nature (practice/habit) because of the kind person that you are (virtue/habit). And it wasn't only Aristotle who argued for these two layers of meaning—it was also the English Puritans. However, the English Puritans would differentiate between the virtue and what they would call an "implanted habit" or a "supernatural habit." The Puritans took the idea of virtue from Aristotle and theologized it. When the Puritans said "supernatural habit," that was a reference to the character of a person. And they believed that if someone is truly virtuous, God planted those habits in him or her (Jer. 31:31-33).

> Habit (as Action) = Regular, frequent practice (automaticity)
> Habit (as Virtue) = Character, disposition, implanted/
> supernatural habits

BIBLICAL DEFINITION OF HABIT

Take a look at the following verses, which can help us to understand how habits are defined in the Scriptures:

+ But solid food is for the mature, for those who have their powers of discernment trained by constant practice to distinguish good from evil. (Heb. 5:14)

---

8   Aristotle, *Nicomachean Ethics*, trans. C.C.W. Taylor (N.P.: OUP Oxford, 2006), 2.

- Not neglecting to meet together, as is the habit of some, but encouraging one another, and all the more as you see the Day drawing near. (Heb. 10:25)

- They have eyes full of adultery, insatiable for sin. They entice unsteady souls. They have hearts trained in greed. Accursed children! (2 Pet. 2:14)

Notice that those passages use the terms "practice," "habit," and "hearts trained," which all mean something along the lines of "a usual or customary manner of behavior." Jesus is said to have a custom/habit of going to the Mount of Olives (Lk. 22:39). Those are the same kind of frequent practices that Aristotle and the Puritans spoke of—when you do something so regularly that it becomes second nature to you.

When the Bible speaks of character, it also uses the classical term "virtue." Second Peter 1:5-11 explains how to have assurance that you are a true Christian, and for that to happen, Peter says that you must first "supplement your faith with virtue" (v. 5). Then he adds six more character traits we should be developing, and concludes by saying, "Therefore, brothers, be all the more *diligent* to confirm your calling and election, for if you *practice* these qualities you will never fall" (v. 10). Peter says that character is formed by diligent practice, which is another way of saying we must work hard at developing godly habits.

…character is formed by diligent practice…

WHO SAYS WHAT?

As mentioned at the beginning of this chapter, Aristotle stated that "it makes no small difference, then, whether we form habits of one kind or of another from our very youth; it makes a very great difference, or rather all the difference."[9] He described habit as something that inclines a person, somewhat like when a round rock is thrown up a smooth incline. Yes, we can throw that rock a far distance, but inevitably it will roll back down. It does so because it is inclined to do so—literally! Thus, Aristotle would say that a person will act in accordance with their character. We as Christians obviously cannot fully agree with Aristotle's perspective of people and habits, because truly good habits are only developed when God transforms your heart. People will act contrary to their former nature when God changes their nature. But Aristotle's teaching is significant because it shaped later Christian perspectives on habit.

For instance, Thomas Aquinas would imbibe Aristotle's perspective and teach the same thing in his *Treatise on the Virtues*.[10] Aquinas said that habits are both virtues and frequent actions, using the same idea that the frequent act will increase the virtue. He also continued what Aristotle started by describing the importance of habits as both descriptive and reflective—descriptive in that a person will act in accordance with his or her virtue and reflective in that the habit will reveal the virtue. So, Aquinas and Aristotle were buddies in their perspectives on habits, both suggesting very similar things.

The conversation about habits among Christians went somewhat dark until the English Puritans wrote on the matter. What's interesting is that the English Puritans were also influenced by Aristotle, even quoting him in regard to the matter of habit (calling him "The Philosopher"). What the English Puritans did, however, is talk about habits in a more theological way—showing that God changes a person's heart, which in turn changes a person's habits. Like Aristotle, they also said that the habits are reflective and descriptive—reflective of the character of a person, and descriptive of what habits a person should possess. However, the Puritans called for habits to be developed—like most modern teachers do. In fact, the Puritans' emphasis on spiritual duties was one of the reasons that they were called "Puritans" in the first place.

---

9   Aristotle, *Nicomachean Ethics*, trans. C.C.W. Taylor (N.P.: OUP Oxford, 2006), 1103b, 25.

10   Thomas Aquinas, *Treatise on the Virtues* (Englewood Cliffs, NJ: Prentice-Hall, Inc, 1966).12.

It wasn't until the modern era—beginning with William James, the father of American psychology—that we now have a wider variety of perspectives on habit. As with most of our beliefs about people, modern theories on habits have a body-first perspective. Some make habits entirely physiological, like James and Charles Duhigg, modern authors and teachers who wrote a book called *The Power of Habit*. The Puritans, however, would take a more "developmental" approach and argue that although your body can learn to act without much intentionality, your mind and heart are still ultimately in the driver's seat of habit development.

THEY ALL SAY IT'S IMPORTANT

Whether you agree with the Puritans or with Duhigg, you must recognize that all those who have spoken about habits have also spoken of their importance. If habits are something that molds virtue, as Aristotle argued, then that makes perfect sense. Modern Christian literature is somewhat weaker in this regard—it has spoken mostly about the *how* of habits and not about the *why*. In other words, we've said, "Develop these habits," rather than, "Here's why you should develop these habits." But even though there are varying perspectives on the importance of habits, all the literature across the ages agrees that they are indeed important. Listen to the words of William James:

Modern Christian literature is somewhat weaker in this regard—it has spoken mostly about the how of habits and not about the why.

> [Habit is] the enormous fly-wheel of society, its most precious conservative agent. It alone is what keeps us all within the bounds of ordinance, and saves the children of fortune from the envious uprisings of the poor. It alone prevents the hardest and most repulsive walks of life from being deserted by those brought up to tread therein.... It is well for the worlds that in most of us, by

the age of thirty, the character has set like plaster, and will never soften again.[11]

If you have read William James, you know that as a Christian there is much to disagree with. He often attempts to take what is distinctly God's—the soul, for instance—and seeks to understand and explain it without the Bible or consideration of God. This alone makes his writing dangerous for the undiscerning. Yet, when James made this particular statement about habits, it seems that he was more right than wrong. Habits do form and confirm, and as James also said, by the age of thirty, most people are who they will be because of what they habitually do.

But there must be something more to habits than the "plaster effect," right? James paints a somewhat hopeless picture of the future of a person if the wrong types of habits are developed early in life. And there are certainly times where a person's habitual poor decisions continue to heap trouble upon their life—poor communication, angry explosions, terrible money management, and so forth. But the Bible speaks of change as possible, real, and present.

Through the resources that have been made available in the death of Jesus, God's Son, a person is never "plaster;" rather, the Bible says that we are clay in the hands of the Potter.

Phew! That brings hope. No matter what kinds of habits you have developed, there is a possibility of change. But William James is highlighting an important reality when he says that what you repeatedly do shapes the type of person you will become. This is nothing other than character formation. Character formation is where, from our childhood, we are developing character traits through practice. Character formation is the type of person you become or are becoming because of how you live your life.

---

11   William James, *Writings, 1878-1899* (New York, NY: The Library of America, 1992), 145.

INWARD, OUTWARD, AND UPWARD EFFECTS OF HABITS

Imagine that every weekday, you wake up, get ready for the day, and then go to the homeless shelter in your community to serve breakfast. From 7:00 a.m. until 8:30 a.m., you wash dishes, serve breakfast, sweep the dining room, and greet the guests at the shelter. After a while, you no longer need to set your alarm—you wake up, get ready, and head off. Over time, you become mindful of the shelter in the rest of your life. You see sponges while you're shopping at the grocery store and think, *The shelter needs a few more dishwashing sponges*, so you grab a few for the shelter. You swing by the hardware store for a home project and see that they have brooms on sale for a great price. You grab a few brooms to take to the homeless shelter next time you go. The character trait of kindness or consideration (i.e., mindfulness of others) is developed through your habit of going to serve at the homeless shelter. It's not rocket science. You became a kinder and more considerate person because you habitually served at the homeless shelter. That's what it looks like to have your character formed through habits. Every day, we see this scenario play out in one way or another: we habitually do things, and those things form or de-form character in us. And this is part of what makes habits so important.

Daily functioning is another reason habits are important, as we learned in Chapter 1—God has designed people so that they can learn something with automaticity and perform that function with very little thought. Even as I type these words, I am demonstrating habit. As you read these words, you are dem-onstrating habit. From walking, to driving, to getting dressed, all the way to chewing our food, we are people who have habits that help us perform daily functions. And that's a good thing. We would be lost without the ability to auto-matically remember how to chew food. That could get dangerous very quickly! Habits help us to act without much thought once we have acquired them. In fact, it's not a stretch to say that without habits, there would be no daily functioning.

Character formation and daily functioning are what habits do within us, which we could call the inward effects of habits. But what can habits do for others (the outward effects)? Part of the purpose of this book is to help you to leverage godly habits for the good of others, which *can* and *should* be happen-ing in your life. I mentioned the example of serving at the homeless shelter, and there are many other ways that your habits can do good for others in your social sphere (we will discuss the different spheres of life in a later chapter). Some people have excellent relational hab-its and thus have a very dynamic social sphere around them—for instance, those who remember names when you first meet them. Remembering people's names is a simple way of demonstrating

Part of the purpose of this book is to help you to leverage godly habits for the good of others

that you care for them—so is calling people on their birthday to remind them of how thankful you are for them. Or consider the habit of being a good lis-tener. When we speak with good listeners, they aren't checking their smart watch. They aren't watching the television. They aren't reading a book. Rather, they are looking at us, tracking with us, repeating what we say, asking clarifying questions, and really seeking to understand what it is that *we* are saying. Good listeners have developed a habit of not being distracted while they talk to oth-ers, and it comes across in very pleasant and well-received ways.

Your habits can bless others and actually prompt them to be more like Jesus. In this way, your habits are not only of the utmost importance to you but also to those around you. You can, even unintentionally or without much thought, be a kind person to those who are around you. You have developed the practice of cleaning up after yourself, so your co-workers are blessed when they borrow the company van after you. You have developed the habit of waking up when your alarm goes off the first time, so your room-mates or spouse bless your name on high! The importance of habits does not merely tell us that every so often we should do something nice for oth-ers. No, it's that we should live our lives daily and constantly for the good of other people—so much so that it becomes a part of the fabric of who we are. Generosity is a part of us. Kindness is a part of us. Serving others is a part of us. When the character trait of kindness meets daily functioning, much good can be done to others through our habits.

And finally, what about the upward importance of habits—the way that habits affect our relationship to God himself? Well, we would be remiss to fail to mention that when we do good to others, perform daily tasks faith-fully, and develop certain character traits, all of those should be part of our worship for God. "For from him and through him and to him are all things, to whom be glory forever" (Rom. 11:36). In fact, God is glorified when we do all those things. So, when developing your daily habits, do so with an eye to please God (2 Cor. 5:9). The Bible says that even when you are eating and drinking—even the minutest of daily functions—that you should do so to the glory of God (1 Cor. 10:31). That is the upward importance of habits. John Owen said the way you can tell the difference between a merely moral habit and a godly habit is that the end of every godly habit is "the glory of God in Jesus Christ."[12] This includes everything from the practice of our habit to the reason why we develop that practice in the first place.

Can you imagine how wonderfully pleasant it would be to habitually do what glorifies God? To do what God wants you to do with relative automaticity? You habitually trust him. You habitually meditate on truth. You habitually speak to others in God-glorifying ways. And so forth. My desire is that God would work in your life to the point that glorifying him will be on autopilot! That will be the way we live in a glorified state when we are in the presence of God: habitually obedient to the Father. So we could say that godly habit development is God's kingdom coming on earth as it is in heaven. Habits are of vital importance because you can, in a very real sense, habitually glorify God.

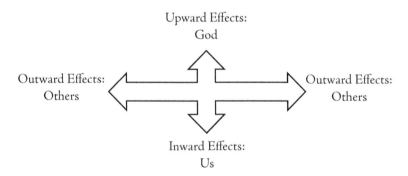

Upward Effects:
God

Outward Effects:
Others

Outward Effects:
Others

Inward Effects:
Us

FIGURE 1: Inward, Outward, and Upward Effects of Habits

Figure 1 is simply a way of helping you remember that there are inward, outward, and upward effects of habits.

---

12 John Owen, *The Works of John Owen*, vol. 3 (Carlisle, PA: Banner of Truth, 1965), 503.

IMPORTANT, YET NOT DETERMINATIVE

As we discussed in Chapter 1, although destructive habits may seem compulsory, there is no bad behavior to which a Christian is enslaved in the sense of not being able to escape it (Rom. 6:11, 1 Cor. 10:13). As a Christian, because of the power of God in your life, you are never truly "stuck." You have hope for change because of his promise to form you into the image of his Son, Jesus Christ (Phil. 1:6).

This is why I like to say that habits are "seemingly determinative" (rather than "determinative"). Being influenced by our habits and being enslaved to them are two very different things. You are not a slave to anything as a Christian because God has given you a new heart with which you can truly and authentically cry out to him as "Abba Father" (2 Cor. 5:17; Rom. 8:15). Because of your union with Jesus and the Holy Spirit indwelling you, you now have all the riches of God's blessings in your life (2 Cor. 5:15, 21). In fact, the Bible suggests that if you are unified with Jesus by faith in him, the only thing that you have been "determined" to do is to become more like Jesus (Rom. 8:29). Jesus is the perfect image of God, the Father, and the exact imprint of God's nature (2 Cor. 4:4; Heb. 1:1-2). Your habits can tug against that work of re-conformity to the image of Jesus, but your habits cannot determine who you are. In fact, if you truly are a Christian, you have been "determined" to reach that goal, because God promises to complete the process of sanctification by working in you to do his will (Phil. 1:6, 2:12-13).

You cannot even continue in long-term sinful habits of living, because you are God's child and he will lovingly discipline you to bring you back to holiness (1 John 3:6, Heb. 12:3-11).

> *Rejoice in the fact that God will not abandon his children, nor leave them to their own devices*

Rejoice in the fact that God will not abandon his children, nor leave them to their own devices. Yet still recognize the potency of habits while experiencing the freeing grace of God. Your habits are of paramount importance because of the way they affect you, your relationships to others, and—most importantly—your relationship to God.

CHAPTER 3

IT'S ALL
ABOUT THE HEART

Books on habits usually talk about habit development, types of habits to develop, and maybe something regarding the benefits of developing habits. You can read such books by business leaders, entrepreneurs, sociologists, and the occasional Christian. Yet very few speak to the reason why we want to develop good habits in the first place. Almost all the literature focuses on the habits themselves, not the motivation we should have. It seems to be a blind spot in habituation theory. Some will speak to habits that help you be more efficient and productive. But, as Christians, we recognize that some things we do may seem inefficient but are still God's will for our lives. For instance, Philippians 2:3-5 says we should put others' interests above our own. What if acts of kindness for others on our part cause us to lose a significant amount of time and money? Does that mean we shouldn't do those things? We cannot be people who are motivated first by efficiency and productivity. Neither of those should be the chief motivations for our lives. Rather, we must be motivated by an over-arching desire to please God. That desire is at the center of biblical habit formation.

THE HEART OF THE ISSUE

A key thrust of this book is an emphasis on the heart. Some of you may have picked up the book looking for specific steps on habit development, but weren't as interested in learning about motivation theories or the reasons why we develop habits. Motivations are important, however, because we all have them—it's just a question of whether they are good or bad, helpful or unhelpful. We may be motivated by vocational preparedness or success. We may be motivated by a dissatisfaction with who we presently are. But we all have motivations that come from somewhere and shape the types of habits that we develop.

The Bible speaks to the reasons why you do the things you do—even in regard to why you develop habits. It suggests that you do the things you do because of what is taking place inside of your immaterial heart. The heart has been defined in this way:

> The heart is the governing center of a person. When used simply, it reflects the unity of our inner being, and when used comprehensively, it describes the complexity of our inner being—as composed of mind (what we know), desires (what we love), and will (what we choose).[13]

To put it simply, the heart is the control center of our lives, influencing all that we do.

Proverbs 4:23 says, "Keep your heart with all vigilance, for from it flow the springs of life." We are people who are living out the attitudes of our inner person. Over and over again, the Bible teaches the centrality of the heart in all that we do. When Jesus speaks of the source of your words, he uses the analogy of a tree. He says that bad words are much like bad fruit on a tree (Matt. 12:33). Most likely, if you would see bad fruit on one of your trees, you wouldn't think to yourself, *Let me run down to the grocery store, buy some new fruit, and come back to pin it to this tree.* (We wish it was that simple!) What you would do is think about things like the nutrients in the soil, the amount of sunlight the tree is receiving, and how often you water the tree. You know

...the heart is the control center of our lives, influencing all that we do.

---

13   A. Craig Troxel, *With All Your Heart: Orienting Your Mind, Desires, and Will Toward Christ* (Crossway: Wheaton, IL, 2020), 21.

there is something taking place at the root level that is causing this bad fruit. Likewise, when you see rotten speech, you cannot merely think to yourself, *Let's learn a new vocabulary.* No, you must understand what Jesus meant when he said that "out of the abundance of the heart the mouth speaks" (v. 34). The reason why we have word problems is that we have heart problems. It's the heart that overflows with speech, so to borrow the terminology of Proverbs 4, you need to "guard your heart."

In another instance, Jesus speaks about the centrality of the heart when it comes to behavior. In Mark 7:21-24, in regard to ceremonial cleansing and what truly defiles a person, he says, "From within, out of the heart of man, come evil thoughts, sexual immorality, theft, murder, adultery, coveting, wickedness, deceit, sensuality, envy, slander, pride, foolishness. All these evil things come from within, and they defile a person." Jesus' disciples are accused of eating while being ceremonially unclean. Yet, Jesus says that external things do not defile a person, but that which comes from the heart. The heart is at the center of all that we do.

This understanding of the heart is essential to a right understanding of habits. Your habits cannot make a heart of stone or a heart of flesh. Only God can do that, and he promises to do so for those who are Christians (Jer. 31:33). The New Covenant, of which Jesus is the Mediator (Heb. 9:15), includes the promise that God will change his children by giving them a new heart. This new heart comes with new motivations, new desires, new affections, new loves, and new volitions. God changes you from the inside out when you become his child. While an exhaustive discussion of the dynamics of the heart is not the goal of this chapter, you must know that the source of what you do is found in your heart.

God changes you from the inside out when you become his child.

SUPERNATURAL AND IMPLANTED HABITS

To the Puritans, the heart was not only a part of the discussion regarding habits—it was *the most important part.* Their terms "supernatural habit" and "implanted habit" emphasized the role of the heart. John Owen, chaplain to Oliver Cromwell, wrote this: "In the sanctification of believers, the Holy Ghost doth work in them, in their whole souls, that their mind and wills, and affections, a gracious supernatural habit, principle, and disposition of living unto God, herein the substance or essence, the life and being, of holiness doth consist."[14] Notice that Owen referred to heart change as a supernatural habit. In defining habits as frequent practices that we learn with automaticity, we should include in those practices the "dispositions" or heart attitudes that incline a person to the frequent practice. Those dispositions are what the Puritans called supernatural or implanted habits.

John Flavel, another Puritan, suggested that the fear of the Lord is an implanted habit. The Holy Spirit creates that holy reverence in the heart of Christians so that we will want to please God in our lives.[15] This is heart change that leads to change of action. If we asked the question, "Why do you fear the Lord?," the Puritans would say that it's because God has changed your heart!

The goal of this discussion is not that you would start to use terms like "implanted habit" or "supernatural habit" in daily conversations—I don't want you to get ejected from your next dinner party! Rather, the purpose is to learn that *the reason why you develop habits is more important than the development of habits itself.* And the only acceptable life-dominating motivation is a motivation to glorify and please God, as we discussed in the last chapter. Sure, you can have sub-motivations like money, rest, peace and quiet, or an enjoyable job. But more than anything, *the desire to glorify and please God is what must drive habit development.*

DESIRES

The heart functions in various ways. Sometimes the Bible refers to it as the source of loves, thus Jesus declares the only acceptable form of love for God is with your entire heart (Matt. 22:37), echoing the words of the *Shema* (Deut.

---

14 John Owen, *The Works of John Owen*, vol. 3 (Carlisle, PA: Banner of Truth, 1965), 2.

15 John Flavel, *The Works of John Flavel*, vol. 3 (Carlisle, PA: Banner of Truth, 1982), 252.

6:4-10). Yet the Bible also speaks of thoughts of the heart—for example, "every intention of the thoughts of his heart was only evil continually" (Gen. 6:5, cf. Heb. 4:12). In other places, the Bible speaks of the heart as being the center of desires and says that, as you continue to grow in sanctification, God changes what you want (Ps. 37:4; Phil. 2:12-13). While we cannot understand everything about our hearts, of course (Jer. 17:9), we can get a pulse on some of what is happening inside us by asking questions like these:

+ What do we want more than anything?

+ What do we love?

+ What do we honor above all else?

+ What is it that we ultimately aspire to?

+ What do we daydream about?

+ What is our motivation to get out of bed each day?

Our desires are so important to understand because they drive us to take action. The Bible does not condemn all desires, of course, and it says that some are commendable. In I Timothy 3:1, for instance, Paul says that "if anyone aspires to the office of overseer, he desires a noble task." He is commending the desire to be an overseer, not rebuking men with that desire or saying they should suppress it. When Jesus told the Pharisees that their desire was to

...it wasn't the fact that the Pharisees had desires that was problematic for them; it was the orientation of those desires.

do the will of Satan (John 8:44), that was a direct indicator that they did not have a new heart (v. 47). Again, it wasn't the fact that the Pharisees had desires that was problematic for them; it was the orientation of those desires.

As Christians, we should be people who have desires for God and desires for what God wants. Having received a new heart at the moment of conversion, we recognize that we are to have one reigning desire, which is to please

God. As Paul says in 2 Corinthians 5:9, "Whether we are at home or away, we make it our aim to please him." The Apostle Paul was motivated by one dominating desire in his life: to make much of Jesus (Phil. 1:27; 1 Cor. 10:31). This desire to please God is the one that should order and structure all other desires in our lives. It is this desire to please the Lord that informs what we should and should not desire in the first place! Wayward, sinful desires are so wrong because they crowd out the desire to please God and keep us from living it out (James 1:13-15). Oh, that this life-dominating, reigning desire would permeate all of our lives—especially habit development!

If you desire to invest in relationships this year, please do so because you want what God wants. If you desire to become more efficient this year, please do so because you want to please God more. If you desire to advance your career this year, please do so to the glory of God. May you be able to say with the Apostle Paul, "I count everything as loss because of the surpassing worth of knowing Christ Jesus my Lord" (Phil. 3:8).

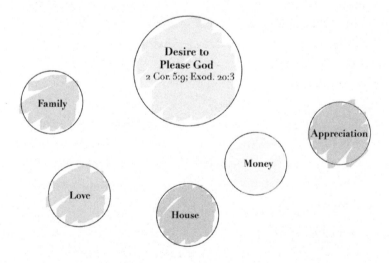

FIGURE 2: Comparison and Relationship of Desires

DESIRES AND IDOLS

It's important to understand how our desire to please God should relate to the other desires in our lives, like our desires for family, house, love, appreciation, kids, marriage, and yes, even money. Figure 2 represents those various desires with smaller circles. You are free to desire all of these things, as none of them are inherently sinful—even money. Paul said that "the laborer deserves his wages," so don't be cheap when paying your employees (1 Tim. 5:18)! Yet, Paul also said that "the love of money is a root of all kinds of evils. It is through this craving that some have wandered away from the faith and pierced themselves with many pangs" (1 Tim. 6:10). You can legitimately desire for your boss to pay you in a way that honors God, but you can also desire to be paid in a way that dishonors God. When you desire money more than you desire to please God, the Bible calls that idolatry (Exod. 20:3, Col. 3:5). As Jesus said, "You cannot serve God and money" (Matt. 6:24).

This is why all the other circles in Figure 2 are smaller than the one representing a desire to please God. Your other desires should never become "bigger" than that one. Your desire for money, for instance, is only legitimate when that desire stays smaller than your desire to please God. Ken Sande, in his book *The Peacemaker*, describes three criteria for how we can know if something has become an "idol" in our lives:

+ **Sin to Get It**: We know that we are desiring something too much when we are willing to sin against God to get that thing we are desiring. It doesn't mean that the desire is inherently sinful, because we can desire something good and sin to get that good thing (i.e., appreciation).

+ **Sin to Keep It**: Sometimes we know that what we have is good and we will do whatever it takes to keep this thing, including sinning against God. Relationships are an example of this: we desire a relationship so much (good thing) that we will stay in a sinful relationship that we know dishonors God (sin to keep).

✦ **Sin if We Don't Get It**: When we don't get what we want, we lash out in sinful responses. Whether we are pouty for the next three days or explode in sinful bursts of anger, we didn't get what we desired and now are sinning as a result.[16]

Look back at Figure 2. When our desires for family, money, a house, appreciation, or love get bigger than our desire to please God, then we have committed idolatry. How can we know our desires have grown too big? Well, we ask ourselves, "Am I willing to sin to get it, sin to keep it, or sin if I don't get it?" Those are good barometers of where our heart and its desires are.

Now let's connect the dots specifically to habit development. You can, and should, desire to be productive and organized, for instance. But your desire for productivity and organization can get too big in your life. When you are *not* being productive and you respond in a way that pleases God, that shows your desires are in the right place. If you're ultimately desiring to please God, then you'll respond by bearing the fruit of the Spirit—even when not getting what you immediately want (Gal. 5:22-23). However, if your desire for productivity has grown too big, your failure will result in impatience, unkindness, and a lack of gentleness—all of which are antithetical to a Spirit-filled life. So, if that happens, should you scrap any kind of desire to be productive? No! You should repent of your idolatry and then seek God's help in not letting your desire for productivity get bigger than your desire to please him.

When we understand the relationship of heart and habits, we are free to be the most productive, physically-healthy, relationally-connected, and vocationally-successful people we can be! Let's develop dynamic businesses to the glory of God! Let's get fit this year to the glory of God! Let's have deep and meaningful relationships around us for the glory of God!

It's heart and habits, not heart *or* habits.

---

16   Ken Sande, The Peacemaker: A Biblical Guide to Resolving Personal Conflict (Grand Rapids, MI: Baker, 2004), 100-15.

CHAPTER 4

THE HOLY SPIRIT IN HABIT CHANGE

The importance of the Holy Spirit's role in habit change cannot be overstated. Any good book on habits must wrestle with the proper emphasis regarding human effort and the work of the Holy Spirit propelling that effort. He seals the Christian (Eph. 4:30), indwells the Christian (1 Cor. 3:16), guides the Christian (John 16:13), and comforts the Christian (John 14:16)—along with many other important contributions. All those works of the Spirit, in one way or another, relate to our habit development. The Holy Spirit is helping believers to live lives of holiness, and we can't do that without godly habits. Not all habits have direct impact on our holiness, sin, or sanctification, of course, like the habit of driving your car. But any spiritual fruit in the Christian's life is a direct result of the work of the Spirit in producing that fruit (Gal. 5:22-23). Furthermore, without the work of the Holy Spirit in a person's life, there can only be change in "moral habits," as John Owen would call the external works of law-keeping that even unbelievers can practice. But without the Spirit, there can never be a true, God-pleasing change of habits in the heart.

THE HOLY SPIRIT AND THE CHRISTIAN

Christians come from many different backgrounds. This affects everything, from the type of church that you attend to the way that you disciple your kids. Despite our variegated backgrounds, however, all true Christians share the same basic beliefs about the nature of God the Father, God the Son, and God the Holy Spirit. We can all rally around the fact that God is one God, yet there are three persons of the Godhead: Father, Son, Spirit. We all believe that.

Our diversity begins soon after that, however. How exactly does the Holy Spirit seal us? At what point? What does it mean for him to guide us? When does he baptize us and what does that bring with it? And so forth. This chapter, however, will focus on the things we can all agree on about the work of the Holy Spirit, and how they pertain to habit development.

THE HOLY SPIRIT'S ROLE IN HEART CHANGE

As I said earlier in the book, the Puritans used the term "supernatural habit" to describe what takes place when a Christian's heart is changed. John Owen said this:

> There is wrought and preserved in the minds and souls of all believers, by the Spirit of God, a supernatural principle or habit of grace and holiness, whereby they are made meet and enabled to live unto God, and perform that obedience which he requireth and accepteth through Christ in the covenant of grace, essentially or specifically distinct from all natural habits, intellectual and moral, however or by what means soever acquired or improved.[17]

In other words, the obedience of believers is actually caused by the Holy Spirit, from the very beginning of our Christian lives. When a believer starts the process of following Jesus, even the desire to do that is indicative of the Holy Spirit's work.

The Holy Spirit is the heart changer! At the moment of salvation, he takes the dead, cold heart and regenerates it so that it pumps with spiritual life. In accordance with the promises of the New Covenant, the Holy Spirit changes the control center of a person so that he or she wants to live a life

---

17   John Owen, *The Works of John Owen*, 3.6.

pleasing to God. Then the Spirit continues that work until you meet Jesus in the next life (Phil. 1:6). If you have an impulse to sit down and read your Bible because you want to hear from God, for instance, that desire is an evidence that the Holy Spirit has been at work in your life. Hopefully you can see the relevance of this to our habits—we won't develop a God-glorifying habit of Bible reading unless the Holy Spirit has first changed our hearts. It's really that cut-and-dry: if the Holy Spirit doesn't change your heart, you won't desire the right things.

"INDUCING TO COMPLY"

Jonathan Edwards wrote, "As to the gracious leading of the Spirit, it consists in two things: partly in instructing a person in his duty by the Spirit, and partly in powerfully inducing him to comply with that instruction."[18] Imagine you're standing in the middle of a trampoline. You have a soccer ball that you keep kicking toward the edge of the trampoline, but it rolls right back down toward you. "Inducing to comply" means that the Holy Spirit creates an inclination toward good inside of us. So, when we find obedience attractive, we should thank the Holy Spirit for his work in our lives. When obedience is habitual, that's the work of the Holy Spirit.

> *...if the Holy Spirit doesn't change your heart, you won't desire the right things.*

This inducement (like the sanctification it produces) is both "initial" and "progressive"—it happens at the moment you became a Christian and also during the further steps of obedience. You don't see Jesus as beautiful until the Holy Spirit reveals him to you, and that happens at the moment of salvation (2 Cor. 3:17). When you first started following Jesus, the Holy Spirit showed Jesus to you. And when you beheld Jesus, in all his glory, you saw him as beautiful.

---

18   Jonathan Edwards, *A Treatise Concerning Religious Affections in Three Parts* (Grand Rapids: Christian Classics Ethereal Library), 285.

But the Holy Spirit continues to work in your heart and makes obedience look attractive to you. As you "keep in step with the Spirit," your desires are changed from what you naturally wanted before you were a Christian and you are able to "live by the Spirit" (Gal. 5:25). In verse 24, Paul also says, "Those who belong to Christ Jesus have crucified the flesh with its passions and desires." The Holy Spirit takes the work of Christ on the cross and applies it to you by placing you in union with him (Rom. 6:1-11).

So, when you think to yourself, *I really need to be a better communicator with my family because that's what God wants me to do,* pause and recognize the Holy Spirit has put that conviction and desire in your heart. He is the one both inducing and enabling us toward obedience in God. He might be using tools like this book to refine pockets of your life, but he is still the one doing it. When you've learned to habitually use edifying speech with your adult children, even when disagreeing with their life choices, remember that you are doing so because of the work of the Holy Spirit. That way God gets all the glory!

THE HOLY SPIRIT'S WORK IN THE CHRISTIAN'S EFFORT

There is a synergistic relationship between the work of God and the works of the Christian. If you are a Christian, the Bible is clear that you are called to live out your faith in Jesus through obedience. The Epistle of James says that we should have certain fruits that correspond to our faith, otherwise it is dead (James 2:18). James teaches us about the kind of faith that saves us, while Romans and Galatians teach us that faith alone saves us.

Good fruits are part and parcel of what it means to be a follower of Jesus. In fact, Paul told Titus that the reason Jesus saved us was "to purify for himself a people for his own possession who are zealous for good works" (Titus 2:14). And he later added, "I want you to insist on these things, so that those who have believed in God may be careful to devote themselves to good works" (Titus 3:8). Have you paused to think about what

Good fruits are part and parcel of what it means to be a follower of Jesus.

you're most devoted to? Perhaps it's work, or family, or hobbies? But Paul says we should be characterized by a devotion to good works. That devotion comes from the work the Holy Spirit has done in our life. Just a few verses earlier, Paul makes it clear that the Holy Spirit has breathed new life into our dead hearts, and we are to do our work in light of his: "He saved us…by the washing of regeneration and renewal of the Holy Spirit" (Tit. 3:5).

Only by the work of the Holy Spirit can the Christian work. Yet the Christian still works. The Holy Spirit gives us the spiritual energy we need to work. He gives us the spiritual nutrition that our spirit needs to exercise itself. But we still must exercise ourselves for godliness (1 Tim. 4:7). What I hope you're hearing is this: just because the Holy Spirit has changed you, that doesn't mean you should be passive, lacking diligence. No, rather, we have been saved to be zealous for good works—persevering, striving, sacrificing, and breaking a spiritual sweat for the sake of good works. The Holy Spirit doesn't use your *non-effort* to transform you—he uses your effort. He works through your effort.

Remember what Thomas Watson said: "What I have spoken is to encourage faith, not indulge sloth. Do not think God will do our work for us while we sit still. As God will blow up the spark of grace by His Spirit, so we must be blowing it up by holy efforts."[19] Knowing the role of the Holy Spirit in the Christian's life should push us toward greater action, not inaction. You're crouched next to the fire, taking massive gasps of air and blowing on the embers to stoke them into a flame that can only burn by God's power. You're the vehicle that is easier to turn while it's moving. It could be possible to lift a vehicle and move it inch by inch. But to push the vehicle is the easiest way to steer it. Your growth and change are the movement of the vehicle, while the Holy Spirit steers you. He steers as you move.

Don't let this discussion make you uneasy. At this point you might be picturing a person that you'll never be and don't want to be. The overachiever, up at 4:30 a.m., running marathons and drinking way too much coffee. You don't have to become "that person" to change your habits. And

---

19 Thomas Watson, *The Godly Man's Picture* (Carlisle, PA: Banner of Truth, 1666), 237.

don't let this be where you offer an excuse for why you can never change your habits. Like Thomas Watson said: "This shouldn't make you a couch potato." Or…something like that. No! Don't accept that answer from yourself! You *can* change because of the Holy Spirit's power. It's not how awesome you are or how organized you can become—it's how much the Holy Spirit can work in your life.

THE FINE BALANCE OF BOTH/AND HABIT DEVELOPMENT

It's very important to emphasize both God's role and our role in the development of godly habits.

Imagine, as your morning begins, you wake to spend some time reading the Bible. That's your habit. Now, at this particular moment, you're struck by the things you're reading. God convicts you that you need to seek forgiveness from your neighbor for how you rattled off some condescending words the other day. It's hard for you to read the part of the Lord's prayer that says, "Forgive us our debts as we also have forgiven our debtors" (Matt. 6:12). But you wouldn't have seen that verse without your habit of Bible reading. And God has now used that habit to bring conviction to your heart.

Paul asked the Corinthians, "What do you have that you did not receive?" (1 Cor. 4:7). Good question, Paul. I can't think of a whole lot, can you? We can't even make our physical hearts beat, let alone cause the supernatural change we need in our spiritual hearts. That's the point. *The Holy Spirit* has given you the heart that wants to wake up and read the Bible in the morning. He then applies the truth of the Bible to your heart. And he convicts you that you need to talk with your neighbor. That's how it works. And it all started with your habit of Bible reading.

> We can't even make our physical hearts beat, let alone cause the supernatural change we need in our spiritual hearts.

Multiply that times two quadrillion and you'll start to get a sense of how often that kind of process is working its way out in your life. Many habits and combinations of habits are used by the Holy Spirit to bring about big change in your life. So, don't get lazy and don't think you did it all. Rather, make the changes you need to make with God's help.

Be careful not to err on either side by an over-emphasis or under-emphasis on the Holy Spirit's work. Pray for his help and trust in his power, but also work hard. Really hard. Harder than anyone, like the Apostle Paul says he did in 1 Corinthians 15:10. In that verse it seems a bit of braggadocio for him to say, "I've worked harder than any of them." But notice that he makes sure to add, "Though it was not I, but the grace of God that is with me."

CHAPTER 5

INWARD EFFECTS
OF HABITS

I grew up in the church; that might not be a shocker for you. My father was a church leader and I found myself imbedded in Christian communities—often against my will! AWANA, Youth Group, Sunday School, and other legitimate and meaningful programs within our local churches would know that they had at least two participants: my sister and me. The pendulum often swings for those in thoroughly Christian contexts between "your actions are everything" to "your actions aren't very meaningful." I've experienced the vacillating of this pendulum in various seasons of my life.

Before we were Christians, our "religious" habits—memorizing the Bible, going to Church, sword drills, etc.—were changing us, even though those changes may have been unknown to us. Prior to true conversion, however, those habits tend to form self-righteousness rather than a dependence on Jesus. Furthermore, we often wrestle with thinking our good habits are in some way meritorious to our salvation. But your habits can never make a lick of contribution to your salvation. Only Jesus can do that. Your habits are only filthy rags compared to the absolute holiness God demands (Isa. 64:6; Eph. 2:1, 8-9).

When I was young, I felt the tension of "being good" yet needing a Savior. We know our good habits don't earn us the grace of God, but they are still desirable habits. The pendulum swings in the opposite direction when we slip toward "hyper-grace" and think that God's grace will cover it all, regardless of whether we repent or not. Hyper-grace emphasizes that you just need to "love God" and all else is well. There's a lack of emphasis on obedience, persevering in your faith, and abiding in Jesus. Rather, we just need to "let go and let God." He's got us. Our actions aren't that significant when the pendulum swings toward hyper-grace, so we exploit our Christian liberties and fail to pursue good works as we should.

When accompanied by the work of the Holy Spirit, however, good habits become a means of helping us to cultivate spiritual appetites. Thomas Watson said, "There are two things that provoke appetite. Exercise: a man by walking and stirring gets a stomach to his meat. So by the exercise of holy duties the spiritual appetite is increased. 'Exercise thyself unto Godliness.'"[20] Good habits are like eating when you know you should. Sometimes you're sick, and you really don't have an appetite. Deep inside, however, you can hear the voice of your mom telling you to eat some crackers and they'll help you feel better. Or in the morning, we would rather sleep a little longer, but we know that we need to wake up and spend some time in the Bible. We have to force-feed ourselves the Word sometimes, but it's for our own good. It doesn't earn us more love from God to wake up and read the Bible, but we know we need to do it to be spiritually healthy.

It doesn't earn us more love from God to wake up and read the Bible, but we know we need to do it to be spiritually healthy.

I have alternated from an extreme habit-obsessing type to a poster child of hyper-grace, from judgmental older sibling in the family of God to freewheeling entitled younger sibling. But neither option is acceptable. Your habits are never going to make you right with God. Only Jesus can do that. Yet, you still need habits to produce their effects in your life. To veer toward hyper-grace misses the point that there is value in your habits. To over-emphasize habits without heart leads to a deluding self-righteousness. Understanding the effects of habits biblically can keep us from these extremes.

20   Thomas Watson, *The Beatitudes* (Carlisle, PA: Banner of Truth, 1660), 134.

PRESENTATION PROBLEM VS. PRECONDITIONING PROBLEM

Most of us don't think too much about our habits...until something goes wrong. We spend every day practicing our habits, but don't always know what habits we have and even the effects of those habits. It's often when something goes wrong that we stop and ask, "Hey, why does this keep happening?" And those who never pause to ask questions like that are the toughest nuts to crack, because they never consider what they may be doing in a habitual way to contribute to the problem. It's common for us to do things without knowing exactly how they work: use computers, fly in airplanes, drive cars, or parent our children. (Only partially kidding about the last one!) Most of us use a computer or smartphone every day, yet not many of us could describe how those devices work with specificity. We just use them, and they just work. That's all we really care about in the end...until something goes wrong. That's when we begin to wonder and ask, "Why does this keep happening?" That's when we fire up YouTube and watch instructional videos on what went wrong.

Habits are like that. Have you ever wondered, after another bad breakup in a relationship, *What's the matter with me?* Or perhaps you struggle to maintain close social relationships outside of work and think, *Am I doing something wrong here?* You get let go from another job and ask yourself, *Am I a bad worker?* Those kinds of problems have often been referred to in counseling as "presentation problems."

A presentation problem is what we think the problem is, or what we see as problematic.[21] A bad break up, for example, is a presentation problem, but it's not the real problem. There are layers of problems that have contributed to the presentation problem, and we must peel back those layers to understand the nature of the real problem. One of those layers is the "preconditioning problem." A preconditioning problem is where we have developed long-term habits of responding to a situation in a certain way. Preconditioning problems are habits we have developed. So if the presentation problem is

---

21   Jay Adams, *The Christian Counselor's Manual* (Grand Rapids, MI: Zondervan, 1973), 249-52, 436.

a bad breakup, then the preconditioning problem could be how we handle conflict, what we expect in a dating relationship, or how we normally deal with our anger. Those are long-term patterns that are the underlying causes of our presentation problems.

An example of this would be a person who has no meaningful relationships. Imagine someone who is in his mid-50's, keeps to himself, and doesn't have strong family ties or community of any sort. He definitely isn't dating anyone and complains of being lonely or that nobody cares about him. That's not to say he is a social leper, but he is just not close with anyone, and he's now starting to feel it. As this lifestyle progresses, he is experiencing more and more desire and need for others to be a part of his life (especially on moving day!). As Christians, sooner or later we realize that we *need* the church. Having no meaningful relationships is a presentation problem, but it is the result of something else going on in our lives.

The preconditioning problem in this instance could be the relationship skills that a person has or has not developed.[22] A habit in the social sphere of life is a way of relating to others that has become almost second nature. Communication is a great example of this. In the above example, if the person who has no meaningful relationships has minimal communication skills and, worse yet, is a hurtful communicator, that has probably stymied relationships and caused them to remain surface-level. This could include even basic skills like calling or texting people back. Those skills contribute to good relationships—not to mention more significant communication skills like listening, not talking over people, and not having to get the last word in.

If that's true, then when we have no meaningful relationships around us, we should ask ourselves and others, "What bad habits are contributing to this problem?" I'm not talking about a single instance here, like when it's about one friend only, but when it's a pattern in our lives. So, as a counselor, when I meet people who complain of loneliness or no meaningful relationships, I cannot merely say, "Well, let's find you a friend." That may be part of the solution, but I need to go deeper and say, "Let's make you into a person

---

22 For a great description of relationship skills, see Ernie Baker's *Marry Wisely, Marry Well* (Wapwallopen, PA: Shepherd Press, 2016).

who is friendly. Let's make you a person who is a good friend." That kind of transformation of the heart and character (i.e., desiring to please God by being more friendly) will always bear good fruit in social relationships.

As I said, we often don't think about habits until something has gone wrong. Perhaps that is why you are reading this book. In God's kindness, he has shown you that something is not as it should be, so you are now seeking to grow and change. In that case, problems are a means of helping us grow to be more like Jesus—if we use those problems to evaluate how we need to change. When we see prob-

...we often don't think about habits until something has gone wrong.

lems in our life, God can and does use those problems to grow us to who he wants us to be—more like his Son, Jesus. So, don't be discouraged if you sense a problem that needs to change. Keep going in this book, so you can understand more about habits and specifically (in the rest of this chapter) how they affect your life. Let's talk more about the categories we mentioned in Chapter 2.

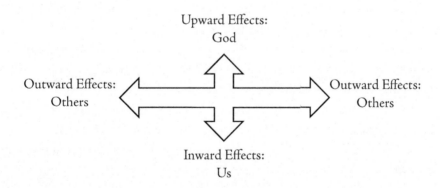

FIGURE 3: Inward, Outward, and Upward Effects of Habits

INWARD EFFECT #1: DESIRES ORIENTED

The first and most important effect of habits is on the desires of the heart. Christian philosopher James K. A. Smith spends a great deal of time in his books speaking to the formative power of habits.[23] He does so because when you habitually do something, it shapes what you want to do. Consumer behavior experts understand this well—that's why they track what you do online and then, when you are looking at one product, they suggest similar products. Their ads follow you through another three webpages, enticing you to purchase items from the company they work for. Toy store chains send out big catalogues to families prior to Christmas—not because they love children so much and want them to be aware of all the toys that are out there. No, they want our kids to practice the habit of looking through the catalogue because they know that will create desires in them for those toys. It's genius. Sick, twisted genius, but genius nevertheless.

Consumer behavior experts have picked up on the effects of habits—how what people regularly do will often shape what they want to do. You implicitly know this but perhaps haven't paused to think about it much. Consider the effect that a favorite hobby has on your life, something like fishing, painting, yardwork, sewing, sports, or mountain-bike riding. You buy that new bike and the next thing you know, you need new clothes, a new rack for the bike, a watch to track your heart rate while riding, and a million other gadgets that relate to this new hobby. Your habit of riding the bike has cultivated in you a greater desire to ride the bike, and to buy all the bike accessories that go with riding. That's because your habits shape your desires. That's part of James K. A. Smith's point when he writes about "cultural liturgies" that shape what a person loves.[24]

However, Smith wasn't the first to discover this dynamic. In fact, the English Puritans wrote about it almost 400 years ago. Richard Baxter, for instance, said, "If you cannot presently suppress the desire, you may presently

---

23 James K.A. Smith, *Desiring the Kingdom: Worship, Worldview and Cultural Formation* (Grand Rapids, MI: Baker, 2009) and *You Are What You Love: The Spiritual Power of Habit* (Nashville, TN: Baker, 2016).

24 Smith, *Desiring the Kingdom*.

resolve to deny the flesh the thing desired (as David would not drink the water though he longed for it, 2 Sam. xxiii. 15, 17) and you may presently deny it the more of that you have."[25] He goes on to say that if you struggle with covetousness, then you shouldn't go window shopping anymore. And by not going window shopping, you will help suppress the desire for stuff. Conversely, the habit of shopping may be cultivating in you a covetous desire.

Now that's profound! *Your habits shape your desires.* But as much as we appreciate Smith and Baxter, we have to ask whether this is something that is found in the Bible. Does the Bible speak about your habits shaping your desires? First, let's consider these words of Jesus about money and possessions: "Do not lay up for yourselves treasures on earth, where moth and rust destroy and where thieves break in and steal, but lay up for yourselves treasures in heaven, where neither moth nor rust destroys and where thieves do not break in and steal. For where your treasure is, there your heart will be also" (Matt. 6:19-21). Jesus warns against the goal of accumulating riches in this world and demonstrates the fragility of earthly wealth—moth and rust destroy, thieves steal it. Those verses are the most familiar part of the passage. However, notice that Jesus also warns about the *effect* of storing up treasure, whether it's in heaven or on earth. Jesus says, "Where your treasure is, there will your heart be also" (v. 21).

Your habits shape your desires.

Some have taken that verse in a pragmatic sense: "Show me where you spend money and I'll show you what you treasure." Yes, that's obviously true. But Jesus isn't only saying that money serves as a descriptor of your heart—it also serves as a director of your heart. Both are true. One of the results of investing in something is that your heart naturally follows.

The Apostle Paul also illustrates this dynamic when he suggests that the Corinthians had experienced desire orientation through their giving. In 2 Corinthians 8:10 he says, "In this matter I give my judgment: this benefits you, who a year ago started not only to do this work [i.e., giving] but also to desire to do it." The Corinthians were a divided church, with whom Paul had

---

25   Richard Baxter, *A Christian Directory* (Morgan, PA: Soli Deo Gloria Publications, 1996), 284-85.

to work out many doctrinal and practical issues. And as he prepares them for giving to the needs of the Christians in Jerusalem, he commends them for two features of their past generosity: (1) they actually gave and (2) they desired to give. Isn't that interesting? Sounds a lot like Jesus' words on treasures and the heart, right?

Here's the point: the habit of giving shapes what you want to give to. Yes, God gives you new desires at salvation, including the desire to give back to him. But when you regularly give to anything—church, non-profits, animal rescues, missionaries—your heart is inclined even more toward those things. Through your giving, you care more about those organizations and the people in them. You want to support them more and more. You are endeared to them and can't help but think that they need you as a partner in what they're doing. You take interest in their success and concern in their failure. When they get sick, you pray for them. When it's been a difficult year for the organization, you try to help in whatever way that you can. You do all of this because you have made an investment in them.

This is why giving is so important, by the way. It's not because God needs the money and if you didn't give, then God would be put in a tough spot! No, rather, it's the effect that giving has on you: you learn to love well, to be more thoughtful, to share resources, to not love your stuff so much, to be sensitive to the needs of others, to value what God values, and so forth. *Giving shapes you.* Not giving isn't only bad for the organizations that you should be supporting, like your church. Not giving is so bad because you will harden your heart and accumulate treasure only on this earth, and that should terrify you!

Giving is not the only habit mentioned in the Bible that will shape your desires—gathering with the local church is another one. In Hebrews 10:24-25, the author of Hebrews says, "Let us consider how to stir up one another to love and good works, not neglecting to meet together, as is the habit of some, but encouraging one another, and all the more as you see the Day drawing near." The warning is that there are some who habitually neglect to gather with the church and then miss out on the "stirring up" toward love and good works. In order to grow as Christians, we must all "meet together" with the other members of a local,

> *Gathering with the church is a necessary stimulant to love and good works.*

Gospel-preaching church. We must habitually do this, not just on rare occasions or when we're not working. Gathering with the church is a necessary stimulant to love and good works.

You've undoubtedly experienced how gathering with your local church shapes what you want. Our family certainly has. On some Sundays, none of us even want to wake up—let alone get ourselves ready and make the trek to church. Our pajamas are calling us! More sleep is calling us! Football is calling us! But we still go. We go because we've made a habit of going and would feel out of place if we stayed home that day. So, we go, and upon arrival we see some of our good friends. We chat with them for a moment, and then we go hear the Bible preached to us! The sermon was exactly what we needed to hear, and then we see a couple who moved away and is back visiting. We have missed them so much and are encouraged by speaking with them and getting to hug them! God has used us going to church (habit) to help us want to go to church (desire).

Something similar has happened to you, right? On the drive home, you think, "I'm so glad we went to church today!" But that's not what you said at 7 a.m.! You just witnessed how the habit of attending church shapes your desires.

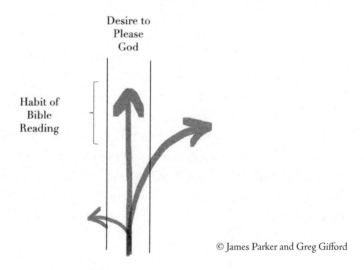

© James Parker and Greg Gifford

FIGURE 4: Oriented Through Habits

Figure 4 depicts how habits shape desires in relation to another practical life issue—Bible reading. It shows how we as Christians want to please God with every aspect of our being, yet we also often have other wayward desires. In the diagram, the arrows deviating to the left and right represent those wayward desires. But a habit of Bible reading—one example among many we could mention—keeps us oriented toward pleasing God and provides course correction for when we don't. Like two guardrails, the habit of Bible reading keeps our desires headed in the right direction. In the times when our desire to please God wanes, we still read our Bible out of obedience to him. Or sometimes we merely read our Bible out of habit! But God uses this habit of Bible reading to orient our desires back to him—to bring us around, so to speak. If we didn't maintain the habit of reading our Bible, then we would deviate away from desiring to please God more and more.

Our very first godly desires are not a result of habits, however, which shows clearly how dependent we are upon God's grace. It is God alone who changes the heart of a person to draw him or her into participation in the New Covenant and grants the new desires promised in the Covenant. It is only through salvation in Jesus that a person can begin to have God-honoring desires in the first place. The snowball can only begin rolling downhill when God tells it to. Yes, you cultivate desires, but you do not create desires. That's God's responsibility. This is evident when we pause to ask the question in the first place: "Why do you want to have godly habits?" Well, you want to have godly habits because God has changed your heart to want to have godly habits. And by exercising those habits (like giving, attending church, and reading the Bible), you further cultivate those desires. In a quote we've already discussed, Thomas Watson likened this to a flame.[26] Watson said that God fans the embers of our desires through our efforts. So, our desires will never change for good through self-indulgence or idleness, but through obeying God habitually. In this way, as the psalmist said, God will give us the desires of our heart (Psa. 37:4).

---

26   The full quote is, "What I have spoken is to encourage faith, not indulge sloth. Do not think God will do our work for us while we sit still. As God will blow up the spark of grace by His Spirit, so we must be blowing it up by *holy efforts*... The smoking flax shall not be quenched, but we must blow it up with the breath of our effort." Thomas Watson, *The Godly Man's Picture* (Carlisle, PA: Banner of Truth, 1666), 237-38.

INWARD EFFECT #2: CHARACTER FORMATION

Will Durant summarized Aristotle by saying, "We are what we repeatedly do."[27] Durant also argued that excellence is not an act but a way of life. This is the historical understanding of habit as virtue. Although we don't typically use the term "virtue" in our modern vocabulary, we do often think of characteristics or character traits. Aristotle said, "To sum up, states [i.e., character traits] arise from similar acts. Therefore, one must ensure that one's acts are of such a kind; for one's states [i.e., character traits]

> If you consistently act generously toward others, then generosity becomes a part of your character.

follow according to the differences of the acts."[28] If you consistently act rudely toward others, then rudeness becomes a part of your character. If you consistently act generously toward others, then generosity becomes a part of your character. So, in Aristotle's words, be careful how you act because that action solidifies the state of who you are.

Simply put:

Habits develop character.

Consider two different individuals. One of them spends the majority of his time working, earning money, and advancing to the next vocational step in his career. Every three to five years, he takes a new job that advances his career and is willing to re-locate for this new position because it advances him individually. Consequently, these decisions end relationships over and over. In fact, before long, this individual stops pursuing relationships with other people because he is focused on his job—not on ministry to others. Church attendance is almost non-existent and the idea of serving at church is almost laughable to him. After all, Sundays are his only day off each week and he has lots of errands to run. At the end of a twenty-year career, this person has become what he's habitually practiced. He is a professional, ladder-climbing, vocational-oriented, high income earner. The thought of turning

---

27   Will Durant Quotes. BrainyQuote.com, BrainyMedia Inc, 2020. https://www.brainyquote.com/quotes/will_durant_145967, accessed January 1, 2020.

28   Aristotle, *Nicomachean Ethics*, trans. C.C.W. Taylor (N.P.: OUP Oxford, 2006), 3.

down a better position for family responsibilities seems almost negligent to him. Volunteering to serve at church would clash too much with the opportunity for a little R&R on Sundays.

Now consider a second individual. This individual spends his time working hard but limiting the hours that he is willing to work due to other commitments like family, church, and friends. Thus, when he's offered a position that will require 50% travel, he automatically declines it. It's a no-brainer because he doesn't want to work more and be away from family and friends, even if his salary would grow significantly. After twenty years of making decisions similar to these, this second person has also become what he has habitually practiced. He works hard, but he also plays hard, and he isn't motivated by the best career move, but by good decisions for his family. To accept a high-paying job that would take him away from his home seems almost negligent. After all, he would not be able to go to church or be around his family enough.

CHAPTER 6

OUTWARD EFFECTS OF HABITS

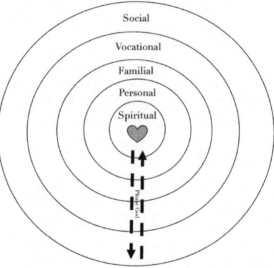

© James Parker and Greg Gifford

FIGURE 6: Spheres of Life

The five "spheres of life" depicted in the figure will serve as a framework for our discussions in several chapters of this book. In Chapter 9, they will be our outline for a discussion of priorities in habit development, and in Chapter 10, we will learn about foundational habits in each sphere. But first, in this chapter, the spheres will aid us in organizing some examples of the outward effects of habits, as we continue to illustrate the importance of habits in our lives and become more motivated to work on them.

EFFECTS IN THE SPIRITUAL SPHERE

The spiritual sphere is the part of our lives in which we relate only to God. This includes issues of the heart, as we discussed in the last chapter, but also includes outward aspects like how you choose to spend your time, energy, and money, and whether those choices are pleasing to God.

We discussed in the last chapter how habits like giving and Bible reading effect our hearts, but consider another example that illustrates how our habits also influence our actions and behavior.

It's not enough to just read the Bible as a regular habit—you should also meditate on it while you're reading it and as you live throughout the day. Imagine, for instance, that you read Matthew 5:44-45 for your devotions one morning: "Love your enemies and pray for those who persecute you, so that you may be sons of your Father who is in heaven. For he makes his sun rise on the evil and on the good, and sends rain on the just and on the unjust." You think about what this passage means for your life practically and you ask God to give you wisdom about how you can live it out that day, then when you get to work you remember what the passage said and pray about applying it at work specifically. Then, Wow! You receive a really snarky email from a colleague and Matthew 5 pops into your mind! Instead of ripping them in return, you decide to respond in kindness. If God can be loving toward his enemies, then you can be too! As a result, instead of ending up in a big fight with your colleague that ruins your day, you feel better because you have done what pleases God, grown closer to him, and been a witness for him. Your habit of meditating on the Word bore fruit in your everyday life.

EFFECTS IN THE PERSONAL SPHERE

While the spiritual sphere of life is where you relate to God, the personal sphere is where you relate to *yourself*. Habits in the areas of sleep, eating, time management, budgeting, exercise, organization, and so forth all have a major effect on the personal sphere of your life.

Consider the habit of exercise, which is one that can shape our lives dramatically. No one is born with the habit of exercising, but everyone can cultivate that habit. Your habit of exercise shapes the health and wellness of your body, which then shapes what you are willing and able to do with your body. For instance, some parents seldom or never engage in physical "play" with their children—no basketball, soccer, games of tag, bike riding, or even hide-and-go-seek, because the parent is physically out of shape. So, if such parents try to play tag with their children, for instance, they get really tired really fast. The habit of exercise has significant ramifications because an unhealthy body simply cannot do certain things (like play tag!).

No one is born with the habit of exercising, but everyone can cultivate that habit.

Another habit that effects the personal sphere of your life is how much time you are willing to spend on entertainment. For some people that threshold is 1-2 hours per week, while for others it might be 1-2 hours per day. For others, it depends on whether it's football or baseball season. The habit of watching television will have significant effects on you personally, including how much sleep you get, how addicted you may become to it, and even what you *cannot* do because of the television. If you turn on the television after dinner every night and that's how you habitually end your day, then you can write off reading books together with your grandchildren. Or going on a walk with your family. Your nights are full of television and you don't do other things because those other things are crowded out by television. You are really interested in a series on television and that series prevents you from playing a board game with some friends. Not to mention that you are probably sacrificing hours of sleep that would be more valuable than one more episode of that TV series.

Some people haven't really paused to evaluate how their habits are affecting them personally. This is not to say that you are necessarily a bad follower of Jesus because you don't exercise enough or because you watch too much TV. And Jesus died for all our sins, including those and other bad habits you may have developed. God loves us anyway because we are in Christ, and he knows that we love him in return. But even those of us who authentically love Jesus can often use a tune-up of our habits, which will then shape who we are and what we are able to do for him.

EFFECTS IN THE FAMILY SPHERE

Within the family sphere, prioritizing family time is a habit that you must develop or suffer severe consequences. You must have some internal mechanism to determine when it's okay to be apart from your family and when it's not. I currently have a family with young children and I know when I am gone too much, whether it's for work or ministry—and if I don't, my wife will surely tell me! If I made commitments to being gone for work or ministry every night of the week—and I could—that habit could get me in big trouble. On the other hand, the habit of saying no to other opportunities so that we can eat dinner as a family four nights a week is one that has brought great blessing and stability to our home.

Another important habit for the family sphere is that of communication. For all the dangers of modern technology, it can be a blessing for married couples who want to develop good habits of communication. Because of cell phones, couples can call, text, and instant message each other all throughout the day for brief updates and questions here and there. Unlike in the old days, for instance, husbands and wives can actually talk when one or both are on the way home from work—though hopefully they're not texting when driving! Conversely, if a couple did not communicate at all throughout the day, did not know when each other was going to be home, and had no clue what was taking place that evening, that would also significantly affect their family.

For all the dangers of modern technology, it can be a blessing for married couples who want to develop good habits of communication.

The habit of frequently communicating with a spouse has great importance for building trust and loving each other. Some families function as roommates until one leaves and others seem like a brotherhood or sisterhood—maybe even a gang! Those are direct results of the habits that you have developed in the family sphere.

EFFECTS IN THE VOCATIONAL SPHERE

Sometimes you'll hear that a person has "a good work ethic" or is a "hard worker." These compliments come to those who have developed certain habits at work. An example of this is when a person makes a habit of coming to work on time. That habit is something that you learn, not something that you are born with. Getting to work on time also implies that you have planned your morning well, sought to be intentional about what time to wake up, set multiple alarms, and planned for traffic, all so you can arrive at work when you should. These habits then affect your work performance and perception by others while at work. On the other hand, if you are often late and erratic in the time you show up for work, it will hinder your performance and negatively influence others' perception of you.

Sometimes people are referred to as "highly organized" as if they have a super-power of organization, a trait that others could never possess. But in reality, such a person has simply developed habits of organization. Filing emails, organizing to-do lists, maintaining a calendar, keeping a workspace clean, and so forth are all examples of habits in the vocational sphere. These habits, like timeliness, are not innate. We learn them and cultivate them for the purpose of being better employees. It is expected of employees that they can manage their email account well, and that they can maintain a professional calendar. A boss is going to get very irritated very fast if he has to tell his employees to open their calendars, write down the meeting time, and then set themselves a reminder. And in college, you might be able to get away with not responding to others' messages, but when you are in a career vocation, most bosses won't tolerate you failing to read their emails.

Habits in the vocational sphere often make or break a person's career. As job candidates, disorganized people are simply not as competitive as organized people with the same qualifications. If you forget where you put the customer's payment for their invoice, you may love Jesus greatly, but you just cost the business time and resources! Your disorganization isn't necessarily reflective of a poor relationship with Jesus. But a good relationship with Jesus should help you cultivate better vocational habits: you will be humble, learn from your mistakes, receive corrections from your boss, and try not to make the same mistake twice. And those kinds of habits will make you a better employee (and a better witness for Christ).

EFFECTS IN THE SOCIAL SPHERE

This final sphere is that of your social relationships—friendships, acquaintances, neighbors, colleagues, people you're ministering to, people who minister to you, your church, and so on. The relationships we have in the social sphere are those we choose to have, outside the more "required" ones in the family and vocational spheres. Perhaps it also includes those relationships we would like to have. And in this social sphere, the habits we cultivate can either promote good relationships or prevent them. The "crazy cat lady," for instance, has habits she has developed that have affected her social relationships—or lack thereof. Likewise, the individual who is surrounded by really in-depth, meaningful social relationships also has habits that have contributed to those blessings.

...the habits we cultivate can either promote good relationships or prevent them.

As with the other spheres, the effects of your habits are significant. Think about the time you spend with other people—what we could call the habit of "time together."[29] "Time together" means that you will free up your calendar so that you have time to meet with others. No children's sports taking you away. No overtime, so you can have time for others. And in those times that are freed up, you don't stay home and watch movies, but you intentionally seek to be with other people. People who do that have quality social relationships, people who don't do not—it's that simple. And as we mentioned in

---

29   Ernie Baker has a wonderful book on pre-marital counseling in which he talks about "Investing in the relationship through time spent." *Marry Wisely, Marry Well* (Willowollpen, PA: Shepherd's Press, 2016), p. 96.

regard to the other spheres, habits of communication are obviously a key in this one. Not communicating with a friend is a sure way to end a friendship. Imagine that you have some friends who are visiting from out of town, and they let you know that they want to grab lunch while they're in town. "Yes, that's great!" you reply. "I look forward to seeing you!" However, once they come into town, you don't answer their phone call or respond back to their text messages. That will be devastating to the friendship.

CONNECTIVITY OF HABITS

As I said I would at the beginning of this chapter, I've used the different spheres of life as a way of organizing examples of the effects of habits in our lives. But I wouldn't want you to get the impression that I'm saying there is no overlap of habits from one sphere to another. This happens all the time, of course, and it provides one final group of examples to show us how important habits are.

Your relational habits affect all the spheres of your life, of course, but so do your habits of daily functioning. Tidiness is an example of the latter. If you are a messy person, then wait until you go to college and spend a semester with your new roommate. Whose shirt is that? Where did your shoes go? What's that smell? Your habits of daily functioning

Your habits of daily functioning often have a ripple effect.

often have a ripple effect. The initial impact, when we are young, is primarily on ourselves in the spiritual and personal spheres of life, but then we go to college and our habits start to affect others. Then later they become issues in marriage and on the job.

After locking my keys in my car twice, I had to develop a new way of keeping track of my keys. Thanks to Pop-a-Lock and two $75 fees, I was determined to never again lock the door and close it without keeping the keys in my hand. So, I worked hard on a new habit and now, when I lock the door of my car, I always have the keys in my hand—even if I use the fob. Hopefully I will never again have to experience the frustration and embarrassment of being about to go on a date with my wife and realizing that I've locked the keys in my car. The babysitter is sitting inside with the kids, my wife is ready to go eat, and I have to call AAA. My habits of daily functioning were not only inefficient, but they were starting to affect various other spheres of my life.

Take one more example: let's say it's time for you to sit down and have your quiet time. Normally you have thirty minutes in which you can study the Bible and spend some time in prayer. However, as you sit down to read your Bible, you cannot find it! You've misplaced your Bible because you struggle to be organized. Now, you spend ten minutes trying to figure out where you put your Bible. Not  only is this inefficient, but it's impeding your ability to actually hear from God that morning. You might be frustrated that you wasted time, but you didn't only waste time. You also had less time reading your Bible.

Some Thoughts on Legalism

Since I've mentioned several examples of having regular "devotions" or "time with the Lord," this might be a good time to discuss the issue of whether such a practice is legalistic.

Legalism expresses itself in at least two ways. One way is overt and obvious because it simply demands more rules. More observances. More… more…and more. It becomes a taskmaster to which no one can measure up. This first form of legalism results in gross levels of judgmentalism for those who don't measure up and even grosser levels of hypocrisy for those who fake like they're measuring up. Paul says in Colossians 2:23 that a proliferation of man-made rules "are of no value in stopping the indulgence of the flesh." That's because when you complete your requirements, you are standing in your accomplishments rather than in those of Jesus.

The second form of legalism is much more covert and subtle; its rule is to have no rules but rather to simply be "genuine," "real," or "authentic." So, a person says, "I'll do it when I feel like it and not until then, because I don't want to be a phony." He or she thinks, *I would be lying to sit down and read my Bible now*. It's like post-modernism in Christian form. *My heart doesn't want to do that. It would be ingenuine of me to pray for those doing wrong to me because I don't feel that way currently.* The law in this form of legalism is: "Don't do it unless you feel like it."

It's hard to determine which form of legalism is more dangerous. On one hand, there are innumerable laws to which no one can ever measure up. On the other hand, there is a new, singular law of feelings-led inactivity. Both of these forms of legalism wreak havoc on us spiritually because we are the ones setting the standard for righteousness, rather than our God.

To avoid both of those harmful extremes, we must have a clear understanding of the role of obedience in the Christian life. Obedience is demonstrative of God's work in our lives. God was already working in our lives for us to take a step of obedience through faith in the first place (John 15:5). As the book of James says, you obey because you believe (James 2:17). Yet, we also obey so that we will desire what God desires more and more. Those in the second category of legalism mentioned above must recognize that it is through the practice of obedience that God will change what they "feel like doing" (Phil. 2:12-13).

The right kind of godly, biblical habits are a cure for legalism because they are born out of a heart that wants to please God. And those habits keep the heart on the right track through the help of the Spirit of God. When you sit down before work and force-feed yourself the Word of God, you may actually rather be sleeping. Let's be real about this. But you know that you should read the Bible to start your day, so you habitually read it whether or not you feel like it. That habit isn't legalism. That habit is lifesaving. Your spiritual well-being is contingent on a series of habits similar to this example. Don't mistake good habits for legalism.

The illustrations above show how habits are connected and have effects in multiple spheres of life. Here's another: When you stop consuming entertainment by 9:00 p.m., it helps you to go to bed on time. When you go to bed on time, it helps you wake up earlier, which helps you to have a habit of

Bible reading. Now, you finish your exercise and get ready for work. But you also get to work on time, and this chain of blessing started with simply not watching entertainment after a certain time at night.

When your prior night is in disarray, however, it will make your morning congested and off-track. Your efficiency for the morning has been significantly decreased. As we'll learn in the next chapter, efficiency isn't the ultimate goal—pleasing God and serving others is. Efficiency *is* a goal, however. We don't worship efficiency over God, but we don't want to lock our keys in our car every day either. A balanced understanding is that one of the effects of habits is their ability to make our daily functioning more efficient and to maximize that efficiency for the glory of God and good of others.

CHAPTER 7

THE PURPOSES
OF HABITS

Best-selling books like *Atomic Habits*, *The Power of Habit*, or *Seven Habits of Highly Effective People* tell us about how habits can make you more impactful or help you achieve goals. As Christians, we can appreciate many of their observations about the kind of habits to develop and how to do so. But we cannot fully endorse those books because they are missing the most important *purposes* of habits. Almost all books on habits put forward a vision of the good life that looks something like this: "be more productive," "reach your goals," or "advance yourself with good habits." As Christians, however, we know that our lives are not ultimately about efficiency. Our lives are not ultimately about productivity. Our lives are not ultimately about self-advancement, either. Our lives are ultimately about God—and bringing glory to him. Secondarily, our lives are about others—not ourselves. And this applies to our habits, of course, so an essential part of a distinctively Christian understanding of habits is that they aim at glorifying God and doing good to others.

Do you realize that efficiency can actually replace God's role in your life and cause you to glorify God less? Take, for instance, the habit of listening. It's not always the most immediately efficient thing to do, yet God has called us to be good listeners (James 1:19). Now, listening means that we cannot always accomplish our task but that we must pause and take interest in the person who is speaking to us—including the chatty person. You know who I'm talking about: the person who doesn't have a "Reader's Digest" version of the story but likes to give you *every…last…detail!* To be most efficient, you would need to interrupt that person and say, "Thanks for your story, but I really need to get going." End conversation. Walk away. Sure, that would help get you out of the conversation and efficiently accomplish your next task, but you would not demonstrate the care toward others that God has called you to demonstrate. Efficiency is not always the endgame.

Productivity is the twin sister of efficiency. Most would define productivity as something like "the effectiveness of productive effort."[30] However, we as Christians should define productivity as accomplishing what matters most in life. It might not seem productive to stop and listen to someone else, but you have been productive in God's economy, because glorifying God and doing good to others is what matters most.

Our habits are not first-and-foremost to help us be more efficient and productive. Yes, habits can (and should) make you more efficient and productive, but that's not the main goal. When understood through the lens of the Bible, habits are first-and-foremost to help us glorify God and then to do good to others.

FIRST PURPOSE: TO GLORIFY GOD

Because the purposes for whatever we do are so important, let's take some more time to consider the first purpose of developing good habits. The Bible is replete with examples of how our lives are intended to bring glory to God. In Isaiah 43:6-7, for instance, God tells the nation of Israel:

> I will say to the north, give up, and to the south, do not withhold; bring my sons from afar and my daughters from the end of the earth, everyone who is called by my name, *whom I created for my glory*; whom I formed and made. (emphasis added)

---

30   Google Dictionary, s.v. "productivity," accessed April 25, 2020, https://www.google.com/search? q=productivity+definition&oq=productivity+defi&aqs=chrome.0.0j69i57j0l6.2908j1j9&sour ceid=chrome&ie=UTF-8

God created people for his own glory, and this purpose informs all of our lives. As Paul said, "Whether you eat or drink, or whatever you do, do all to the glory of God" (1 Cor. 10:31). Ideally, this information isn't new to you and you are well-versed in how the Bible calls you to glorify God. Even in the daily mundane of life, like eating and drinking, we are called to glorify God. In every circumstance, we should make it our ambition to please him (2 Cor. 5:9).

As Christians, our lives were "re-purposed" at the moment of our salvation. The Bible says that before we were Christians, we were people who lived for our own glory, and ultimately for ourselves (2 Cor. 5:15a). This isn't to say that you were as bad as you could be, but that your pre-Jesus purpose was self-oriented. So Jesus came to save you and give you a new purpose: "He died for all, that those who live might no longer live for themselves but for him who for their sake died and was raised" (2 Cor. 5:15). It could be said, then, that Jesus re-purposed us from us to him.

> As Christians, our lives were "re-purposed" at the moment of our salvation.

"Your Manner of Life"

What if you not only glorified God now and then, but became habituated to glorifying God? What if that purpose became so pervasive in your life that you glorifying God was on autopilot. This is what the Bible means when it speaks of a godly "manner of life." Consider the following verses:

- "My manner of life from my youth, spent from the beginning among my own nation and in Jerusalem, is known by all the Jews." (Acts. 26:4)

- "To put off your old self, which belongs to your former manner of life and is corrupt through deceitful desires." (Eph. 4:22)

- "Only let your manner of life be worthy of the gospel of Christ." (Phil. 1:27)

- "You, however, have followed my teaching, my conduct, my aim in life, my faith, my patience, my love, my steadfastness." (2 Tim. 3:10)

Your manner of life is the "type of life" that you live and is closely related to the idea of character. If we say you live a "full" life, that's a statement about your manner of life. If we say you live a "carousing" life, that's a statement about your manner of life. If you had three words to describe your life, like "stressed, busy, boring," those three words describe your manner of life— your customary way of living. The Christian's goal is to have a manner of life in which glorifying God is such a part of the fabric of our lives that we do it customarily.

The first purpose of habits is that you would glorify God so much so that you don't even give a lot of conscious thought to glorifying God. You just live your life habitually to the glory of God because you've developed a habit of doing so. For instance, consider the habit of gathering with your local church for teaching, fellowship, encouragement, and prayer. At some point you will hopefully have developed the habit of worshipping with your local church every Sunday morning. You're not asking yourself, "Should we go to church today?" No, rather, you simply assume you're going, so you wake up, get ready, and get to church. You are habitually doing what God commands us to do in Hebrews 10:24-25. Now multiply that times a thousand other ways that you can obey God on a daily basis—they can all become second nature to you for the purpose of glorifying God!

God Won't Share His Glory with My Efficiency/Productivity

God told the nation of Israel that he would gather them together, for his glory, and he also told them that he would not share his glory with another (Isa. 42:8). Fundamental to the worship of God as supreme is the understanding that God will not allow something else to take his place in our lives. Whether we call them "graven images" (Exod. 20:3) or "idols," God is passionate about destroying such false gods in our lives so that he will be our only God. First Samuel 13:8-15 provides a great illustration when God tells Saul to wait for Samuel, and that rushing the sacrifice is disobedience to

God.[31] "Getting the sacrifice done" was Saul's goal; receiving a blessing from it was more important than doing what God has commanded. So, he was rebuked and punished when Samuel arrived and said, "Has the Lord as great delight in burnt offerings and sacrifices, as in obeying the voice of the Lord? Behold, to obey is better than sacrifice, and to listen than the fat of rams" (1 Sam. 15:22).

When it comes to our habits, I've learned that God will not share his glory with my own efficiency/productivity (E/P). (I even created an acronym for it so I could be more efficient!) As far as I know, no other book on habits has articulated this important truth: we can worship E/P over God. Every book on habits wants to help you be more efficient. However, this one is proposing that you may need to do some less efficient things in order to glorify God and do good to others—like habits of praying or listening, as mentioned above.

> I've learned that God will not share his glory with my own efficiency/productivity

When we are willing to sin against God in order to be more efficient, we know that we have a problem. E/P might be a by-product of our habits, and often should be, but it's never our ultimate aim. If E/P is one of our goals, then we must say that we want to achieve E/P for the glory of God. E/P should merely be a means of helping us glorify God more. Habits aren't different from any other area of our lives, and all of our lives are "from him, through him, and to him" (Rom. 11:36).

SECOND PURPOSE: GOOD FOR PEOPLE

Jesus made it clear that there are two great commandments in the Christian life: love God and love others (Matt. 22:34-40). It's on this call for love that the entirety of the law and the prophets rest. If you love God supremely, you

---

31 Thanks to Brian Mesimer for pointing this idea out to me as he read the draft manuscript of this work.

will love other people (1 John 4:7). In Romans 15:1-2, Paul says basically the same thing when challenging the Christians in Rome to be like Jesus:

> We who are strong have an obligation to bear with the failings of the weak, and not to please ourselves. Let each of us please his neighbor for his good, to build him up.

How did Jesus treat us? Well, he didn't seek to please himself but sought to put others' interests before his own (Phil. 2:6-10). In the passage above, Paul calls the Romans to emulate Jesus by acting in a way that builds others up. In the context, he adds that we Christians should even give up certain rights we have for the good of our neighbors, like eating foods offered to idols (Rom. 14:21). Paul says something similar in Galatians 5:13-14: "For you were called to freedom, brothers. Only do not use your freedom as an opportunity for the flesh, but through love serve one another. For the whole law is fulfilled in one word: 'You shall love your neighbor as yourself.'"

Doing good to others is the second most important purpose of our habits. We develop godly habits with the goal of blessing people: bosses, family, friends, customers, and so forth. Think about how your personal habits can do good to others, using the example of exercise again. Imagine that you wake up every other day to exercise, and through that habit you maintain a high level of fitness in your life. As a result, you are better able to cope with stress for longer periods of time. Furthermore, you can be more active with your family because you exercise. Your physical fitness doesn't just benefit you—it's a blessing to those around you.

Sanctification and Human Flourishing

The good that we do for others can be divided into two over-arching categories: the good of advancing sanctification and the good of promoting human flourishing. Advancing sanctification means that we can prompt others to be more like Jesus. Ephesians 4 says that, as Christians work together with the gifts and roles God has given them, that we will "grow up in every way into him who is the head, into Christ" (Eph. 4:15). In the next verse, Paul adds that when the church acts in these ways, "it builds itself up in love" (Eph. 4:16).

God wants us to have habits that encourage others along their path to greater sanctification, not those that lay a stumbling block in front of them. Poor habits of communication or conflict resolution not only disrupt their journey to being more like Jesus, but flat out discourage it. Yet, not everyone is a Christian and therefore not everyone is on a journey of becoming more like Jesus. Sanctification for some is at a screeching halt; in fact, it never got started in the first place. But we can still do good for them by practicing habits that promote human flourishing.

By habits that promote human flourishing, I mean those that contribute to wellness, health, order, stability, functioning, and other desirable outcomes for those around us. Some habits that we practice may not contribute directly to the sanctification of others, but they do contribute to their well-being in some way. You might be thinking, "It's all or nothing. Either we are helping them be like Jesus, or we aren't." Well, perhaps. We should authentically desire to facilitate others moving closer to the image of Jesus in their lives. But not every issue is one of sanctification or sin. Consider the habit of keeping trash in a bag or another container in your car, rather than on the floor or seats. I don't think anyone would say that it is a blatant act of sin for a candy wrapper to accidentally fly out of the window or fall out when the door is opened. But if no one secured their trash and that was happening all the time, it would definitely affect the well-being of others. It wouldn't take long for the neighborhood to become a much less enjoyable place for your neighbors and their kids. Another related example would be the habit of picking up trash when you see it on the ground—though your neighbors may not become Christians because of that, I'm sure they would greatly appreciate you doing your part to keep the area clean.

Jesus said that God "makes his sun rise on the evil and on the good, and sends rain on the just and on the unjust" (Matt. 5:45). Since God does

> *Some habits that we practice may not contribute directly to the sanctification of others, but they do contribute to their well-being in some way.*

good to even those who will never believe in him, we can be like him as we "do good to everyone" (Gal. 6:10).

Your habits aren't about you. They're about glorifying God and doing good to others. When you fully grasp that, everything you do takes on a weight of significant meaning. Even a simple habit like throwing trash away can be for the glory of God and the good of others. Whoohoo! Never before did an empty Starbucks cup have such value!

CONCLUSION

Perhaps you started this book thinking that you needed to grow in certain habits for your own sake. Yet, your life isn't about you, and the changes you need to make aren't for you alone either. You have a family, friends, a job, and most importantly, a God that is worthy of your efforts. You may have significant personal habits that need to change, like nutrition and exercise, or others that you want to develop in order to get

a better job. However, the motivation in doing that must be for the glory of God rather than for your own glory. God isn't willing to share his glory—he is the one who gave us the ability to develop habits, and our habits are for him!

CHAPTER 8

THE FORMATION
OF HABITS

I t's time to get to the nuts and bolts of habit development. Earlier in the book, I defined habit as both frequent practice and character, emphasized the importance of the heart and the Holy Spirit, discussed the effects of habits in different spheres of life, and talked about the purposes of habits, among other issues. But we haven't said anything yet about how to develop habits. That's intentional, because I want you to have a proper balance in your perspective on habits. In fact, if you wanted to jump directly to the "how" of habit development, then you probably need to go back and read those first chapters again. And if you only care about the "why" of habits, then you should read the coming chapters multiple times. The goal of this book is *not* to create people who are highly informed theoretically but have really bad habits.

The development of habits isn't always as intentional as you may like— just ask your bad habits how they got there! This isn't to say that we are completely unaware of our habit development, but it does mean that we can develop habits unintentionally. Perhaps there's no better illustration of this than when we were children and our mothers were trying to rid us of poor eating habits. We can distinctly remember mom telling us not to chew with our mouths open, put our elbows on the table, or make a mess. Yet, some of us still do those things!

Your development of bad habits isn't always intentional, but your development of good habits almost always is. You learn how to do things like talk, walk, eat, and get dressed without much thought. However, you don't typically learn how to be organized or practice good relational habits without intentionality, except when you are simply reflecting what others around you have been doing. Perhaps your parents or friends are really good communicators, so you've developed great habits of communication by imitation. We'll talk more about this below in the section entitled "Community."

So, though your habits are not always intentionally developed, changing them for good will usually be an intentional process. This chapter will show you the "how" in regard to the intentional steps or actions that you must take. Of course, before you can implement this process, you must first know what habits need to change. And even if you think you know what habits need to change, they might be merely presentation problems, like I discussed in Chapter 5. So, before you fill out the change worksheets I'll provide for you, I suggest that you go through the inventory questions in Chapter 12. But once we know what habits need to change, how do we go about doing that?

FREQUENT, REGULAR PRACTICE

You will find some extremes if you read the available literature on habits. One such extreme is that habits are entirely physiological. Some writers have argued that you develop habits merely because of some type of neurological pathway within your brain. William James, the father of American psychology, provided an example of this when he wrote:

> An acquired habit, from a physiological point of view, is nothing but a new pathway of discharge formed in the brain, by which certain incoming currents ever after tend to escape.[32]

Charles Duhigg takes a similar approach in his book *The Power of Habit*.[33] This extreme of focusing on the outer man seems plausible but doesn't

---

32   William James, *Writings, 1878-1899* (New York, NY: The Library of America, 1992), 137.

33   Charles Duhigg, *The Power of Habit: Why We Do What We Do in Life and Business* (New York: Random House, 2012), 47.

properly take into account the issue of motivation, which is immaterial. If the brain is forming a new neurological pathway, then we have to ask, "*Why* does it form? What is the role of motivation? And did those thoughts *originate* in the brain, or in the immaterial part of us?" The Bible teaches that motivations, thoughts, and other keys to the issues of life

As Christians, we know that we are not only bodies, so a "body-first" approach to habits is imbalanced.

ultimately come from the heart (Prov. 4:23, 23:7). As Christians, we know that we are not only bodies, so a "body-first" approach to habits is imbalanced.

A second extreme, however, is to neglect the role of the body in habit development. The body has the ability to learn to do certain things with automaticity. Every professional athlete is a great example of how a body can learn to do complex, impressive feats with very little thought and effort. Throw a grounder to a baseball shortstop. Ask a basketball player to shoot a jump shot. Tell the track star to leap a hurdle. Each of these would be quite complex and difficult actions for most of us, but these athletes have habituated themselves to be able to do them more or less automatically. To neglect the role of physiology in habit development is equally erroneous, because we know our bodies can and will contribute to it. If you don't believe that, take a flight to a different time zone and watch the changes in your sleep habits!

The balance between these two extremes is that both the heart and the body are part of habit development. To put too much focus on the body is to err toward naturalism. To neglect the role of the body is to forget that God has made us both body *and* soul. It's not either/or, it's both/and.

Almost every author who has written about the development of habits speaks to the importance of regular, frequent practice. The English Puritans of the 1600s wrote about such practice happening in both body and soul. For instance, James Nichols said, "The act strengthens that good motion and disposition which leads to it, and so makes you more ready for another act; and that disposeth to more acts, and those to better; and repeated acts beget a habit."[34] The good motion of the heart is strengthened by practice in the body.

---

34 James Nichols, *Puritan Sermons, 1659-1689*, vol. 1–5 (Wheaton, IL: R.O. Roberts, 1981), 558-59, vol. 1.

But how long do we have to practice certain thoughts and actions until they become habits? That's a harder question. I've personally heard 60, 75, and 90 days suggested as the amount of time needed. Maybe one of those is true. Others propose a longer duration and still others propose shorter. But it's not really important to know the exact day your regular practice will now become a habit. What's important is that you practice your new habit with regularity.

You may want to know when your habit will become second nature and therefore easier to practice. That's definitely a fair question, but knowing the answer is not necessary to habit development. At what point will you just wake up and get ready to go to the gym? Hmm. It's probably not going to be after the first week, but it might start to feel normal by week three. By week eight you may not even need an alarm—you'll just wake up and start getting ready. That's how it works. Anyone who promises you that a new habit will develop in a specific amount of days isn't basing that on empirical data, but on some experience they've had or some wisdom they've picked up from someone else. Maybe they are right or close to being right. However, what you need to focus on is frequent, regular practice as opposed to setting a particular day as your goal.

You shouldn't say, "All right, Day 65 is my goal and I'm aiming at practicing this for 65 days." Rather, take a look at your week and say, "I'm going to practice this new habit three times every week for the foreseeable future." We're not concerning ourselves with the length of time, but the frequency. The frequency is what helps us to be able to measure our success and allows us to work toward long-term change. This is a shift for some of us. New habits require incremental change, and to go from nothing to everything on a certain day is not realistic. We should focus on the faithfulness and frequency of our practice.

Faithfulness Propels Greater Frequency (fa—>F)

As Christians, we are familiar with the concept of faithfulness because we know about God's faithfulness. God's faithfulness means that "he does all that he says and keeps all of his promises,"[35] and 1 Corinthians 10:13 says

---

35 Wayne Grudem, *Systematic Theology* (Grand Rapids, MI: Zondervan, 1994), 1242.

that "God is faithful." When we are like God in his faithfulness, we do what we say and keep all of our promises, even when we don't feel like it or don't see the results at an expected time. The hallmark of our faith is that we don't base our lives on what we see, but on what we can't see. Paul says in 2 Corinthians 5:7 that we "walk by faith, not by sight." This means that we're not going to let our feelings, our comfort, our pleasure, or any other consideration prevent us from making the changes in our lives that we need to make. God has equipped us with all the resources we need to change, and we are going to be faithful to that process; we *must* be faithful to that process. We must, at times, deny ourselves when starting new habits for the sake of strengthening our good desires, as we discussed in Chapter 5. It's through your faithfulness in frequently and regularly cultivating habits that you are going to want to do it more and more, and for the right reasons.

$$fa \longrightarrow F$$

**Faithfulness propels
greater frequency**

$$fa \neq LoT$$

**Faithfulness doesn't equal
length of time**

FIGURE 7: Faithfulness

For Christians, we can now find great significance in what would otherwise seem to be an unmeaningful habit. Cultivating habits can be an opportunity to grow in faithfulness for the glory of God. So, if you want to develop the personal habit of getting more rest, then you block out time in your evenings to ensure you're going to bed on time. You delay morning meetings as much as possible. Your habit of rest becomes a measure of faithfulness in your life: "I want to sleep eight hours per night for four nights out of the week." You are not letting your rest become a myopic habit focused only on self, but an opportunity to be faithful for the glory of God. You pray, "God, your Word says that you are the giver of all rest (Ps. 127:2), so may you see fit to provide rest to me. May I be faithful to watch less TV this week so I can be well-rested and be a better servant for you. In Jesus' name, Amen."

Tortoise vs. Hare Regularity

You're familiar with the story of the tortoise and the hare, right? I want you to reflect on "tortoise" regularity for a moment—the type of regularity that's not rushed. It's not panicky. It's not frenzied. It's not trying to change the world *today*. This type of regularity says, "I'm going to practice this new habit at least three to four times per week rather than seven times per week." The tortoise regularity is steady rather than quick. Its goals are sustainable and achievable. The long game is the posture of tortoise regularity.

Think of small, attainable steps in your habit development, rather than big, grandiose steps. Let's take exercising as an example again. If you are trying to build the habit of going to the gym in the morning, then start with the goal of setting your alarm and waking up earlier. Do that regularly for a while, even if you don't take the further steps of putting on your exercise clothes and going to the gym on those mornings. Once you're in the habit of getting up earlier, you'll find it much easier to do those things. Start with smaller steps and keep building—maybe you can even begin with some limited, easier exercise at home to get your mind and body accustomed to it.

Hare regularity is the opposite of that: it's frenzied, unrealistic, and not sustainable. Think of the friend who started that ambitious, rigid diet. You probably could predict when it was going to fail. Perhaps you've experienced this personally, where you have great intentions and make significant steps to initiate change, but by week three it all seems to dwindle? Hare regularity says, "I'm going to develop this major new habit seven times per week." Yes, that's obviously a laudable goal, but it rarely will come to fruition. It's

...we are people who usually change progressively in baby steps.

not realistic. This is why many diets will give you "cheat days" so that you can realistically stick to your diet the other days, while having a day to splurge! Hare regularity often doesn't work because we are not people who change instantaneously in seismic ways; we are people who usually change progressively in baby steps.

Tortoise regularity is going to bless you in that you won't be so discouraged in growing and compounding your habits. If you're faithful to do something even two days per week, that's a success. And once you've been faithful to practice a new habit two days per week, then you can move on to three days, and so forth. Don't start with hare regularity, by rushing in with massive goals, but progress to greater regularity. If you try to start with hare regularity, then you might fail and not practice the new habit at all!

COMMUNITY

Community plays an integral part in your habit formation. I was at the gym recently and the advertisement playing on one of the TVs said that if you have set new fitness goals, tell your friends, because having others cheer you on will encourage you to reach your goals. As Christians, we should be well-versed in encouragement and accountability. Part of our walk in following Jesus is to be surrounded by people who will encourage us to be more like him and also will hold us accountable when we don't follow him. The author of Hebrews says that believers are to "encourage one another every day, as long as it's still called 'today'" (Heb. 3:13). It's through involvement in a local church that you are prompted toward good works (Heb. 10:24-25).

So, get others involved in the changes you want to make. Ask your small group to pray for you and encourage you to be faithful in your new habits. Or initiate a new regular meeting with an accountability partner. Make use of apps on your smartphone, email chains, and other social tools to share your goals with others. The principle is that habit development takes place in public.

Habits that form in private can still form. But habits that form in community often form more quickly and consistently. As a friend of mine said,

"The people that you surround yourself with either support or undermine who you want to become."[36]

ENVIRONMENT

When developing habits, we often underestimate the role of our environment. Your environment is simply the people, places, and events that surround you. Whether you realize it, or not, your environment can help you cultivate habits or unlearn old habits. Just think of the following scenarios:

- **Military Basic Training:** At 5:30 a.m. every morning a soldier must be awake, dressed, and standing ready for physical fitness training.

- **College:** The college dorms have "quiet hours," after which all the students typically study or sleep.

- **Restrictive Diet:** One spouse has allergies to certain types of food, so even having those foods in the house could pose a health risk.

In each of those cases, the environment is going to shape the habits that are developed. The military basic training will help cultivate fitness and waking at a certain time of the day. College will help a student be inclined to the habit of studying. A restrictive diet will produce certain habits of eating. All three of these environments will decrease a person's intentionality in cultivating habits. You would have to be intentional to *not* cultivate certain habits when in the above environments.

If you are surrounded by people who wake up every morning and study the Bible, then you will be encouraged to do the same thing. Conversely, if you're surrounded by people who oversleep, you'll be tempted to do so. If you are surrounded by families who have one night per week of family time, then you will be encouraged to have one night per week of family time. Your environment reduces, or increases, your need for intentionality in habit development.

---

36   James Parker, personal correspondence, March 2020, Santa Clarita, CA.

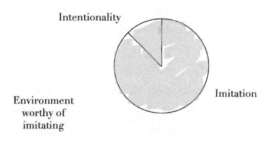

FIGURE 8.1: Intentionality vs. Imitation

Figure 8.1 illustrates the fact that when you have an environment that is worthy of imitation, you don't have to "try as hard" because you will hopefully reflect your environment. This is true because God has made us with the capacity to be image-bearers who are reflectors of him (Gen. 1:27). It's also true because imitation is part of the DNA of who we are, and God uses that tendency in our spiritual growth. For instance, Paul says in Ephesians 5:1, "Be imitators of God, as beloved children." Why do you think it's so important to be a part of a healthy local church? It's because we need an environment worthy of reflection.

Please note that you still need to be intentional, even in the best environment—that's always going to be true. But the need for intentionality is reduced when you are embedded in an environment worthy of imitation. However, look at the next figure:

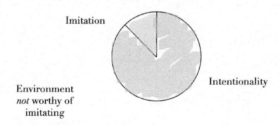

FIGURE 8.2: Intentionality vs. Imitation

Certain environments are not worthy of imitation for a multitude of reasons: they don't honor God, they're hurtful to our families, they're not in alignment with our convictions, etc. Figure 8.2 shows that your intentionality must increase exponentially when you are in a bad environment. There is less to imitate, or perhaps even nothing to imitate. So, when we are in those types of environments, we must work harder to be able to implement our new habits. Our intentionality increases as our imitation decreases. If your college roommates never study, always party, and interrupt you when you're trying to do your work, it will take much more intentionality to develop good habits of study than if they did the opposite.

This could mean that for some of us, a new environment is in order so that new habits can thrive—we need all the help we can get! Maybe we need to look for a new place to live, a new way to spend our free time, a new group of friends, a new way of engaging technology, a new place to shop for groceries, and so forth because we are wanting to engineer our environments to cultivate godliness in our habits. Habits can form in environments that are not conducive, but if possible your environment should be inclining you toward good habits rather than discouraging you.

CHECKLIST FOR THE PROCESS OF HABIT DEVELOPMENT

To utilize this check list, place a check mark in the box when you have completed the designated step, then move on to the next one.

+ **Step 1: Prioritize According to the Spheres of Life**
  Start the process of habit development by forming and evaluating your plan with the proper order of the life spheres in mind. If you aren't regularly reading your Bible and attending church, for example, then plan to start there before you set goals for your vocation.

✦   **Step 2: Identify Specific Habit(s) to Develop**
Once you've prioritized your plan, now identify the habit(s) that you want/need to develop. Think attainability and specificity, and limit yourself to no more than three habits at a time. Start with the spiritual sphere and work outward. Once identified, clearly write out your goals. Examples of this might be "Take an offering check to church every Sunday for a month" or "Family time two nights per week."

✦   **Step 3: Set Frequency Goals (i.e., Tortoise Regularity)**
Your goal should *not* be to practice your new habit daily, but rather the majority of days in your week. Generally speaking, the most you should aim for is five times per week. Your faithfulness at the beginning will propel greater frequency in the future.

✦   **Step 4: Build Community**
Let someone else know about your goals. This can be done via small groups, social media, email, and so forth. Again, the people that you surround yourself with will either support or undermine who you want to become.

✦   **Step 5: Leverage Environment**
Make strategic environmental changes: purge junk food, cancel a Netflix subscription, set reminders, get new friends, change jobs, stop certain hobbies. Your environment should be worthy of imitation as much as you can engineer it to be so. God has made you an image-bearer, so be mindful of what you will reflect in your environment.

✦   **Step 6: Practice!**

CHAPTER 9

PRIORITIES IN HABIT DEVELOPMENT

W e all have birthdays. Some of us would like to forget them, and others would like to make them "month-days." (You know, where all month your purchases are couched in the language of "it's my birthday this month.") We all have experienced the conversation with a co-worker when you learn it was recently his birthday: "Oh, great!" you say, "Happy Belated Birthday. What did you do for your birthday?" And the conversation continues. But it doesn't quite work that way with your spouse. "Oh, great! Happy Belated Birthday" isn't going to appease their wrath! If our co-worker broke down in tears because we didn't call him on his birthday, we'd think, *What's that matter with this person?* But why is this so? It's because you understand that your relationship with your co-worker isn't the same as your relationship with your spouse. Those relationships exist in different spheres of your life, and therefore have different levels of priority.

In this chapter, I'm going to suggest that you prioritize your habit development according to the relative importance of the spheres in your life. Without such a plan based on biblical principles, it's easy to put your emphases and energies in the wrong place and neglect other areas of life that are more important.

Remember, as Figure 6 below illustrates, your heart is at the center of all you do. God changes your heart when you become a Christian, and the newness of your heart permeates every sphere of your life. But some spheres are more important than others, and we need to understand those priorities as we form our plan for habit development. Figure 6 not only shows how the different spheres of life widen out like the ripples caused by a stone thrown into the water, but it also shows how the inmost circles have a higher priority, like a target used for shooting or archery practice.

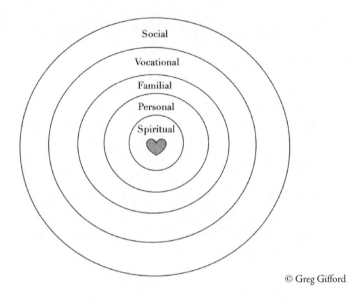

© Greg Gifford

FIGURE 6: Spheres of Habits

God has ordained these spheres and identified what they are, along with the prioritization and relationships between them. God created mankind and assigns various roles to us—like the different but equal roles of a husband and a wife. God has also created relationships for people—relationships with himself, relationships with family, relationships with others. Thus, when you respond to a stranger, you should respond in a way that God has defined for you according to your role. You treat the stranger with kindness and love, in the same way that you would want to be treated (Matt. 7:12). Or perhaps you engage a stranger with counter-cultural hospitality (Heb. 13:2). In those situations, God has created a sphere of life in which your relationship with a stranger fits, and if there is no difference in priority between loving a stranger and loving your spouse (who occupies a different sphere), there is something fundamentally flawed in your understanding. God has defined the spheres and the priorities among them, and understanding both is essential to developing good habits.

WHAT ARE THE SPHERES?

Let's review each sphere, and then we'll discuss the biblical basis for them:

- The **Spiritual Sphere** is where we relate to God the Father, Jesus Christ, and the Holy Spirit—responding to God exclusively in acts of obedience. You could think of this as the sphere of "spiritual disciplines."

- The **Personal Sphere** is where we relate to ourselves in ways that affect our spiritual and physical health. Examples of some habits that are especially important in this sphere are nutrition, sleep, and living on a budget.

- The **Family Sphere** is where we relate to our immediate and extended biological family, in-laws, foster family, adopted family, stepfamilies, or whoever else we would define as family.

- The **Vocational Sphere** is where we relate to others at a job. Your vocation can be part-time, full-time, or contractual.

- The **Social Sphere** is where we relate to others outside of our family and job, such as friendships, dating relationships, neighbors, acquaintances, and strangers.

Obviously the Bible doesn't contain a chart with concentric circles and the names of these spheres, but the ideas behind it are definitely scriptural. For instance, regarding the spiritual sphere, God has created you as a person who relates to him first of all. This identity pulsates through everything that you do—from the fact that you are made in the image of God to the way that you retire, your life is about God. Jesus makes this clear when he speaks of the cost of following him. In order to be true followers of Jesus, we must prioritize him over everything else—a concept known in theology as "the lordship of Christ." Take a look at the following passages, in which Jesus calls his disciples to make him the number one priority:

+ And he said to all, if anyone would come after me, let him deny himself and take up his cross daily and follow me. For whoever would save his life will lose it, but whoever loses his life for my sake will save it." (Luke 9:23-24)

+ Whoever loves father or mother more than me is not worthy of me, and whoever loves son or daughter more than me is not worthy of me. (Matt. 10:37).

Our relationship with Christ must take priority over even ourselves and our family relationships. To truly call him Lord is to confess that he is "before all things and in him all things hold together" (Col. 1:17). He is the center of all other relationships, he is the purpose of our lives, and sharing him with others should be a priority in every sphere of our lives. Conversely, if we were to gain all that this world has to offer but lose a relationship with Jesus, then we have truly lost it all (Matt. 16:26; Luke 9:25).

Since the spheres can be helpful in understanding priorities in our lives, let's take a closer look at each one with that in mind.

SPIRITUAL SPHERE

FIGURE 6.1: The Spiritual Sphere

God has ordained that the first and foremost sphere of our lives would be our spiritual sphere—where we relate to him. We are created to be worshippers of him and him alone. To do otherwise isn't only idolatrous, it's dangerous. To let something take God's place in our lives is foolish treason. This is the indictment of God against the nation of Israel in Jeremiah 2:13:

> Has a nation changed its gods, even though they are no gods? But my people have changed their glory for that which does not profit. Be appalled, O heavens, at this; be shocked, be utterly desolate, declares the Lord, for my people have committed two evils: they have forsaken me, the fountain of living waters, and hewed out cisterns for themselves, broken cisterns that can hold no water.

Not only had the nation of Israel engaged in idolatry, but there was a shocking inferiority to their false gods—they were preferring broken cisterns over life-giving fountains. Unfortunately, we all have a tendency to fall into that kind of false worship, allowing unprofitable priorities to take the place that only God deserves in our lives.

The inmost sphere of Figure 6 is the spiritual sphere because there is nothing weightier, of higher priority, or of greater significance than our relationship to God. Even family cannot take priority over relationship with God. Jesus summarized the law and prophets by saying the greatest commandment was to "love the Lord your God with all your heart and will all your soul and will all your mind" (Matt. 22:37).

This is not to suggest that the other spheres of life are unimportant. It's to say, rather, that there is something *more* important than the other spheres. The Bible also makes clear, for instance, that you cannot be a jerk to everyone around you in your social sphere while thinking that you're doing good in your spiritual sphere (1 John 3:16-18). But the prioritization of your spiritual sphere will propel you into greater effectiveness and fruitfulness in the remaining spheres of your life.

PERSONAL SPHERE

FIGURE 6.2: The Personal Sphere

When we say things like "she has confidence in her abilities" or "he has high expectations of himself," we understand that people relate to themselves in varying ways. You talk to yourself, you think about yourself, you respond to your thoughts about yourself, you have an understanding of yourself, you have expectations of yourself, you have an implicit understanding of your identity, and so forth. Those are examples of dynamics that occur in the personal sphere of your life, in addition to the areas of health and hygiene that I've mentioned before.

Regarding the personal sphere of life, the Bible communicates the theological principle of personal responsibility for faith and obedience. The Bible says there will be a Day of Judgment where we will give an account of things that we *individually* have done in this life (2 Cor. 5:10; Heb. 9:27). From every careless word we speak (Matt. 12:36) to any wrong we do to others (1 Thess. 4:6), we will give account of ourselves to God. This is very personal, because we will give account of our own actions and not the actions of others. Such personal responsibility is both freeing and terrifying at the same time, because we know that we don't have to give account for other people— that's a relief! But we will have to give an account for our own choices (insert scary violins playing!).

The precursor to accountability is knowing what is expected of you. You're not accountable for things you were never told. Many passages in the Bible contain commands that relate especially to the personal sphere of life. Consider, for example, the command to "think about these things" in Philippians 4:8, and "set your mind on things above" in Colossians 3:2. Of course, our thinking affects other spheres of our lives, but it is something that starts and happens entirely within us, often when we are alone.

The way we view ourselves, and otherwise relate to ourselves, is foundational to our relationships to others in the broader spheres of life. So, we need to make sure that we are developing good habits in this sphere even before we tackle change in others. It may not have chronological priority—in other words, you may be working on other habits at the same time. But it should at least be given logical priority over the broader spheres.

FAMILY SPHERE

FIGURE 6.3: The Family Sphere

Family relationships are not as foundational or important as what happens in the spiritual and personal spheres of our lives, but they should take priority over other human relationships in our lives. When I say "family," I'm not referring only to married couples—I'm also thinking of being a child, grandchild, sibling, parent, grandparent, niece, nephew, cousin, and so forth.

The Bible makes it clear that young children are to obey and honor their parents (Eph. 6:1). The Bible also tells adult children that they are to take care of their parents—particularly widows—and make some return to them. In 1 Timothy 5:4 Paul also encourages believers to take care of their widowed sisters, mothers, grandmothers, etc. We are all children, and we know that we have certain biblical obligations to our parents. Whether you have the warm-and-fuzzies for your parents or not, you should prioritize their care in a way that corresponds to 1 Timothy 5:4.

However, there are priorities *within* the family sphere as well. According to Genesis 2:24, the marriage relationship takes precedence over the parent/child relationship. Married persons who do *not* prioritize their own spouses are setting their marriage up for failure. If we treated a total stranger with greater preference than our spouse, it would create significant difficulties, of course. But that mis-prioritization can happen with our children also.

On the priority scale, the family sphere of our lives is below the spiritual and personal spheres but above the vocational and social spheres. This prioritization comes from God, who tells us that no other human relationship is more important than a married couple's commitment to each other (Gen. 2:24, Eph. 5:32). Also, the Bible's commands for children to obey and honor their parents (Eph. 6:1-3) is very different from the commands given to them about their friendships and other relationships in their lives. If a young child obeyed their peers and disobeyed their parents, that would also be a gross mis-prioritization.

In the Bible, we do see that God has called Christians to be hard, reliable, faithful workers (Col. 3:23). But Christians also must balance activities in the sphere of work to prevent them from becoming more of a priority than family. We as adults not only have obligations to our children, but we also still have obligations to our parents, and no job should prevent any of those obligations from being fulfilled.

VOCATIONAL SPHERE

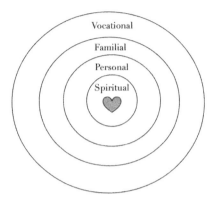

Figure 6.4: The Vocational Sphere

Moving from the spiritual, personal, and family spheres, we now arrive at the vocational sphere. This is the sphere of our lives where we are called to industrious labor by way of our vocation. Most of us work for a living—whether it's part-time or full-time. We must maintain employment for the sake of income. The exceptions to this rule include stay-at-home parents, the disabled, retirees, and those who are in a time of transition, like students. But, typically, employment is part of our daily existence—and that's good.

The Bible repeatedly emphasizes the importance of work. Even before the Fall, Adam was commissioned with the task of keeping the Garden of Eden (Gen. 2:15). This is important because the "pain" of man's labor is a result of the Fall (Gen. 3:17-18), but not the labor itself. Work is part of God's kind plan for mankind to be industrious, profitably engaged, and blessed with fruitfulness. To shirk the obligation to work, whether paid or not paid, is to shirk a fundamental responsibility and privilege of what God has called us to do.

Paul told the Thessalonians, "If anyone is not willing to work, let him not eat" (2 Thess. 3:10). That's a command to work and an explanation of the natural consequences of not working. You're gonna go hungry! The fact that God has called us all to be engaged in meaningful work, however, doesn't necessarily mean that we all will receive a paycheck, or that we are all called to work forty-plus hours per week. But it does mean that none of us are given the license, as God's children, to be lazy or idle. Thus, "whatever you do, work heartily, as for the Lord" (Col. 3:23).

The warning about idleness in 2 Thessalonians 3 provides us with the prioritization of your vocational sphere: after the family sphere, but before the social sphere. What do I mean? The Bible makes clear that to be overly busy with work to the neglect of our families would be erroneous because we wouldn't be fulfilling our God-given role as child, spouse, or parent. And to prioritize social relationships to the point of not working diligently is also erroneous—it's idleness (2 Thess. 3:10).

In Ephesians 5:22-6:4, the commands about family relationships are not only given before the commands about work relationships, but they are more comprehensive and demanding. This shows that family priorities supersede other relationships. Yet, it is also possible for Christians to prioritize family so much that vocational work is improperly neglected. That may have been happening in Thessalonica when Paul wrote, "We hear that some among you walk in idleness, not busy at work, but busy bodies" (2 Thess. 3:11). So, it's important to maintain a balance within biblical priorities.

One more example is the command given to the thief in Ephesians 4:28: "Let the thief no longer steal, but rather let him labor, doing honest work with his own hands, so that he may have something to share with anyone in need." A thief is a burden to others by taking things from them and creating more work for them. However, a hard worker blesses those in his or her social sphere by investing in others. The remedy for the thief is to work hard and to do so in a way that blesses others. That's part of the goal in working on good habits in your vocational sphere—to bless those in your social sphere.

SOCIAL SPHERE

The social sphere of our lives is the outmost sphere in Figure 6.5 and is where our lives intersect with those of others around us: neighbors, church family, friends, acquaintances, and so forth.

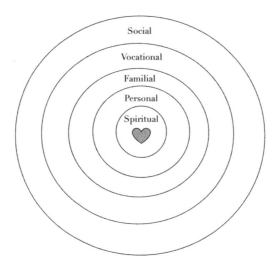

FIGURE 6.5: The Social Sphere

Consider the following types of social relationships that we all possess, and examples of where they are mentioned in the Bible:

+ **Friends**: Proverbs 17:17, 18:24

+ **Acquaintances/Neighbors**: Matthew 22:39; Luke 10:36

+ **Strangers**: Proverbs 6:1, Hebrews 13:2

+ **Church Family**: 1 Corinthians 12:27; 1 John 3:1-3

All these relationships are important, though not as much as those in the other spheres of our lives: spiritual, personal, family, and vocational. But to be faithful to Jesus, we still need to pursue relationships in this sphere. After all, Jesus says that the second greatest command is to "love your neighbor as yourself" (Matt. 22:39). If you were to devote all your time and energy to the vocational sphere and none to the social sphere, you would likely end up as a workaholic with no friends! You are called to engage in meaningful social relationships in which others will sharpen and encourage you and you will sharpen and encourage others (Heb. 3:12-13). These could include older women investing in younger women (Tit. 2:3-4), men training other men (2 Tim. 2:2), or seeking to cultivate friends when moving to a new town. It could include getting to know the people in your neighborhood or helping a church member move.

As with some of the other spheres, there are levels of priority within this one. For instance, Galatians 6:10 says, "So then, as we have opportunity, let us do good to everyone, and especially to those who are of the household of faith." Do good to all others, Paul says, but *especially* other Christians!

PLEASE GOD IN ALL SPHERES

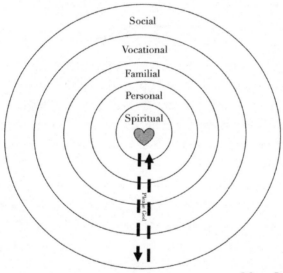

© James Parker and Greg Gifford

Hopefully you noticed the dotted line leading from the heart to the outer spheres. There is also an arrow leading out and an arrow leading back in. It looks like a two-way street. And it is. The arrows are intended to illustrate the reason we should develop habits in varying spheres—because we want to please God. Thus, the arrow going out from the heart illustrates that pleasing God propels us into the spheres of life to develop habits. And the arrow going back into the heart illustrates that our good habits help our hearts want to please God more.

You might remember the climactic scene in the movie "The Grinch" where the Grinch does kind actions for the people of Whoville. The narrator of the movie says, "The Grinch's heart grew three sizes that day!" Then the movie shows a small heart increasing in size to be a larger, healthier heart. In like manner, God increases our desires to please him through our habitual obedience to him (Phil. 2:13). Our desires to please God (the arrow going back to the heart) are increased by our God-motivated habits (the arrow going out).

BIBLICAL PRIORITIZATION OF SPHERES: A CASE STUDY

Meet Harold. He's on the brink of retirement, expecting to work just two more years at his county job. He's employed by the Department of Public Works and has maintained a steady tenure of twenty-five years as a water manager. His vocational habits have been stellar and consistent. He married Nancy in his thirties, and they have three adult children together. Harold has a great relationship with his kids—two out of four weekends every month he is camping, boating, or skiing with the family. At this point in life, he and Nancy will take as much time as they can get with the family, and regularly "nudge" the kids about their desire for grandchildren. It's been Harold's desire to cultivate habits in the family sphere as long as he can remember, and even more so now that he is retiring soon.

Because of the long commutes to work and Nancy's career, they are both only marginally involved in their local church. Nancy works in real estate and often has erratic hours, so it's too exhausting to get home, change clothes, and battle traffic to make it to a mid-week Bible study. Harold and Nancy purchased a larger home on the outskirts of town a few years ago, which almost doubled Harold's commute. Since moving to the new house, they have very little engagement with peers. Everybody has their own thing going and it seems somewhat of a hassle for people to travel all the way out to their new house. This was a surprise to Harold, as the move greatly affected his habits in his social sphere, but long gone are the days when friends would just pop in to say hello.

Losing some of Harold's closer Christian friends has had an impact on his habits in the spiritual sphere. He irregularly reads the Bible, irregularly meditates on Scripture, irregularly listens to sermons, irregularly pursues personal time with the Lord, and so forth. He is currently satisfied with making it to church most weeks, nonetheless, as long as he engages in regular Bible reading before his early commute. While there are currently no crises in Harold's life, it does seem that his relationship with God is anemic and his primary common interest with Nancy is the kids. They've found so much joy in the kids at this new stage of parenting adult children that their own relationship is a bit one-dimensional. Their lives have become lop-sided because of too much priority on their family sphere.

The fact that Harold has postured himself for a great retirement in just over two years helps him grin and bear his job. He's always been a great worker and is ready for his career to be over. Nancy is ultra-supportive of Harold's career and always has been—it just seems that his long-term sacrifices have taken a toll on various areas of his life. She doesn't mind another two years, but wants him to be more involved in church, have his own friendships, and get more time to himself.

As he prepares for retirement, how would you advise Harold to evaluate priorities in the various spheres of his life? He may not be experiencing any obvious crises right now, but some may develop before too long if he doesn't make some changes.

To begin, fill in the blank with the names of the spheres that best match the descriptions on the left, which are listed in order of Harold's priorities. Then note the order of the spheres.

1. Long-term sacrifices for work,   1. _____ Sphere
   long commutes, retirement,
   Department of Public Works,
   Water Treatment Specialist

2. Nancy, three adult children,   2. _____ Sphere
    camping, skiing, and
    boating with kids

3. Church attendance, Bible   3. _____ Sphere
    reading, serving others,
    meditation on Scripture

4. Friends coming to house, lack   4. _____ Sphere
    of Christian friendships

5. Harold's hobbies like   5. _____ Sphere
    camping and skiing, his time
    management in maintaining
    hobbies, or not going out again
    on weeknights.

Now list some ways that you would encourage and challenge Harold about his current priorities. Mention some areas in which he is doing well and others that you see as problematic.

Evaluation of Current Priorities:

1. _____
   _____
   _____
   _____

2. _____
   _____
   _____
   _____

3. _____
_____
_____
_____

4. _____
_____
_____
_____

5. _____
_____
_____
_____

Finally, list some suggestions for how Harold can begin to re-prioritize his life as he prepares for retirement.

1. _____
_____
_____
_____

2. _____
_____
_____
_____

3. _____
_____
_____
_____

4. _____
_____
_____
_____

CHAPTER 10

HABITS IN EACH SPHERE

Now that we've considered proper prioritization, let's discuss in order the types of godly habits that we should be developing within each sphere and why they are so important. This chapter and the inventory in Chapter 12 will prepare you for doing the Personal Growth Worksheet at the end of the book.

Here's a reminder of the order of priorities among the different spheres, which we will follow in this discussion of examples:

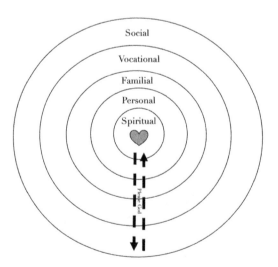

FIGURE 6: Spheres of Habits

SPIRITUAL SPHERE

In the spiritual sphere of our lives, there are some obvious habits that we should seek to cultivate—habits that you've known about for years, but still haven't mastered. Let's consider some of those, along with some others that might not seem to be in the spiritual sphere but rightly belong to it.

Bible reading and meditation. Psalm 1 pronounces the blessedness of the righteous man who delights in the law of the Lord and meditates on it (Psa. 1:2). Reading the Bible and meditating on it throughout your day should be one of the first habits that you seek to establish in your spiritual sphere. You could plan for ten minutes or one hour, but you should make a habit of regularly reading the Bible.

Prayer. Your prayer habits are the conduit of communication between you and God. You pray in the morning during your Bible study. You pray while driving to work. You pray at lunch. You are tempted to get angry with someone, so you pause and pray for God's help to be gracious. Jesus expects that we will be praying (Matt. 6:9-13) and also teaches us that we are the needy child who must bring things to our Father (John 14:13). The habit of prayer is bigger than a prayer list. It's keeping open lines of communication with your Father in heaven. Thus, Paul says, "Pray without ceasing" (1 Thess. 5:17).

Biblical thinking. Only you can take your thoughts captive (2 Cor. 10:5) and set your mind on things that are above (Col. 3:2). In Philippians 4:8, Paul gives a rubric for a pattern of thinking that should become a habit for you: "Whatever is true, whatever is honorable, whatever is just, whatever is pure, whatever is lovely, whatever is commendable, if there is any excellence, if there is anything worthy of praise, think about these things." This habit should dominate your day, so that when you get cut off in traffic, you will automatically apply biblical truth to that circumstance. Not allowing your mind to go wherever it wants can become second nature to you so that you think God's thoughts habitually.

Confession and Repentance. Confession and repentance are integral to walking in the light (1 John 1:5-9). We must confess our sins to God as soon as he reveals them to us and turn away from them toward holiness. "Dear God," we learn to pray, "please forgive me for wanting to be rude toward my neighbor. Help me to love him." You don't even have to think

about it much, you just repent and confess. You make a habit of not har-
boring sinful behavior.

The next few habits may seem to fit more in the social sphere, because
they involve other people. But each one requires a commitment *to the Lord*
in our hearts, so they are necessary habits to develop in the spiritual sphere.

Attending a Local Church. The next habit that you must cultivate in
your spiritual sphere is participation in a healthy, Gospel-preaching church
(Heb. 10:24-25). Every Sunday,
you need to be thinking about
where you'll be gathering with
the church body, not *if* you'll be
gathering. Thus, when you
move to a new town, your habit
of gathering with the local
church will drive you to find a new church. You won't regularly plan weekend
trips away because you have a habit of gathering with a local church.

> *Every Sunday, you need to be thinking about <u>where</u> you'll be gathering with the church body, not <u>if</u> you'll be gathering.*

Serving. God commands us to use our spiritual gifts for building up the
body of Christ (Eph. 4:15-16). You serve other people because you want to
please God, and you can learn to do so out of habit. When someone in your
Bible study needs help moving, you say, "I can help." When you have a habit
of serving others, it becomes part of the rhythm of your life. It becomes a
regular part of your calendar.

Giving of your finances. God loves a cheerful giver (2 Cor. 9:7) and
we are commanded to love God more than money, storing up treasures in
heaven (Matt. 6:20). As we regularly give to the church, missionaries, and
Christian organizations, our hearts become invested in God's work and we
want to give more (Matt. 6:21). And once you are giving regularly, you no
longer even think about whether to use that money for other purposes. You
just give. It's a habit you've developed.

In the spiritual sphere of our lives, we prioritize God by creating certain habits, which then help us to grow spiritually. Through such habits, you
become a wiser person who is more sensitive to biblical truth, ready to turn
from sinful thoughts and actions, and so forth. That's why the Puritans called
these supernatural habits. God changes your heart through your habits and
that change in your heart leads to the development of more godly habits.

This dynamic is most obvious in the spiritual sphere because that's where we relate most directly to God, but it is true in the other spheres as well.

PERSONAL SPHERE

The next sphere of life is where you develop habits that are cultivated by you alone and will benefit you personally. That doesn't mean you should have selfish motives for them, however—the purpose should always be to please God and bless others. Here are some examples:

Time Management. This is the habit that helps you to plan your day, get to appointments on time, understand how long you should be there, and know when to leave. You should have some kind of calendar that you use to budget your time and that you follow pretty closely throughout your day. You will learn and practice details like how long it will take you to get to and from your events or appointments and how much preparation you'll need to do for them. These might seem to be basic skills, but you'd be surprised at how many people are unintentional with their day and it just kind of slips away.

Time management is the management of your most vital resource, which is, of course, time. The Bible teaches that the Christian is to redeem the time (Eph. 5:16). Don't fritter it away on unimportant or meaningless pursuits. Economize and prioritize your time for the sake of Jesus and the good of others, like he did, and he will reward you with "Well done, good and faithful servant" (Matt. 25:21, which is part of a parable about being wise with our resources).

Sleep. Have you thought about how many habits are related to sleep? Every night you have a sense of when it's "too late" and you need to go to bed, and that comes from habits you've developed. You either set an alarm to get up at a certain time or you don't. Maybe you just wake up without an alarm, which can only happen because of deeply ingrained habit. In our technological era, with various screens beckoning us in the final hours of our day, it takes serious discipline to develop healthy sleep habits.

The wheels fall off in the other spheres of your life if you fail to develop proper sleep habits.

Go to bed on time. Go to bed with enough time to wind down and fall asleep. Refuse to waste more time on your phone before you do. And budget enough time to be well-rested. Good sleep habits are something only you can develop, but you absolutely must. The wheels fall off in the other spheres of your life if you fail to develop proper sleep habits.

Exercise. When you hear "exercise," I don't want you to think of working out two to three hours per day. Rather, you should think, *How am I exercising my body to be an apt vessel for God's use?* The Bible recognizes the value of physical exercise (1 Tim. 4:8) and you should too. Just remember that even if it's only a twenty-minute walk around your neighborhood, taking the stairs instead of an elevator, or just signing up for a gym membership, you are cultivating the habit of exercise.

Exercise provides you with greater ability to perform well in other spheres of your life, like the family, vocational, and social spheres. Those who are unwilling to get in shape usually cannot go on bike rides with their families. Or they depend on others to help them because they are undisciplined with their exercise habits. The habit of exercise, on the other hand, helps you to be a more apt participant in your family, a better worker who can manage stress, and someone who is less dependent on family and friends because of poor health.

Nutrition. Trust me, I love burgers and onion rings. But we should all know that we cannot have burgers and onion rings for breakfast, lunch, and dinner. Good habits of nutrition mean you understand proper serving sizes. You understand the nutritional content of different foods. And then you eat the proper amount of the right kind of food according to your body size. That all relates to your diet, but it doesn't necessarily mean specialized "diets." A good habit of nutrition is about you eating a certain way *all* the time. It isn't primarily about losing weight either, even though habits of nutrition usually affect our body weight. There are no foods that are inherently wrong (1 Tim. 4:4), or diets that are inherently right. But you still need to have a plan for what types of food you will eat, and how much of them, and then practice your plan habitually.

Financial Budgeting. All of us are stewarding certain amounts of income. Some of us are stewarding small amounts and others much larger amounts, but we are all responsible to have good financial habits. These include habits of spending, saving, giving, investing, etc. Not developing good habits of money management could be disastrous in your life!

Just as with exercise and nutrition, there are myriads of plans available for how to manage your finances, but the point is that you *must* have some kind of plan for managing your finances—daily, weekly, and monthly. Your habits in this area of your life significantly affect other spheres of your life—good financial habits will bless you and poor financial habits will haunt you. In some ways it's admittedly easier to live on higher levels of income, but your level of income will not determine whether you have good or bad financial habits. You can earn $50,000 or $500,000 a year, but if you don't have good habits, you'll squander either of those incomes.

Recreation. An important part of your personal sphere is taking time for rest, relaxation, and rejuvenation. In Western cultures, we get weekends, holidays, and vacation time to help us recuperate from our work. Habits of recreation could include activities like camping, knitting, beach, boating, traveling, or whatever you find helpful in balancing the rhythms of your life.

Most of us recreate daily or weekly, at least. That means in the evening, after work, you have a time of unwinding from your day. Very few of us work from the moment we wake up to the moment we go to sleep. This habit of recreating is an integral part of your personal life—working too much can cause significant problems. But the converse is true as well. If you've ever come back from vacation so exhausted that you need another vacation, you know it didn't accomplish what was needed in your life. You're tired and now you have to go back to work. You need a break from work every now and then, but only every now and then.

Some of you picked up this book with personal habits in mind. Good. You should develop such habits with proficiency. Every New Year's Day (at least) should prompt an audit and re-structuring of your personal habits. But this is a good place to remind you again about the purposes of habit development, because we are often tempted to do this in our personal sphere for selfish reasons. And this is where most books on habit take you: to improve you, work on you, accomplish your goals, be a better you, etc. But remember that the Bible says to put others interests before your own and to do nothing from selfish ambition (Phil. 2:3-5). Even in things like sleep, exercise, and nutrition, you should have the mind of Jesus, who put others' needs before his own. We should want to be rested, for instance, so we can better serve our families or our customers. Just because it's a personal habit doesn't mean that you are the only person it is for.

When someone doesn't rightly prioritize personal habits, it affects the remaining spheres of life in a negative way. An example is something that happens to Christian workers on a regular basis—ministry burnout. This often occurs because people neglect the personal sphere of their lives for the sake of serving others. There is a good desire to "give themselves up" for their ministry, but in the process, they give up necessary habits like rest, nutrition, or exercise. And that lack of prioritization takes its toll over time. Such brothers and sisters are going to break down—eventually—if they do not prioritize the personal sphere over the social sphere. Again, please don't see this as selfish, because the purpose is to help ensure that we are glorifying God and doing good to others. In ministry contexts, good habits in the personal sphere will help you serve others better *over the long term*. Personal habits are not primarily about you. In the above example, those "burned-out" believers shouldn't stop serving others, but should ensure that they are getting enough rest, eating well, and exercising so they will be able continue and excel more at serving others.

FAMILY SPHERE

The family sphere comes after the spiritual sphere and the personal sphere but before the vocational sphere. God has ordained that we should prioritize our families more than our jobs, but not more than him and our own spiritual health.

Habits in this sphere are those only you can develop that pertain primarily to your family. Let's consider the following examples of some of the most important ones.

Time together. The habit of spending time with your family is one that you must cultivate—it won't happen on its own, particularly when life gets busy. Evenings, special occasions, weekends, or other regular times must be set aside for this purpose, and it must become a habit of life. This means you are managing your personal time so that you are free to be with your family at such times. Time together is a matter of quantity as well as quality, though the amount of time will vary according to the situation. The habit you develop may only be thirty minutes before you go to bed, but all good family relationships require some kind of intentional investment in this regard.

Consider two examples of time together: date night with your spouse and hang-out time with your kids. You might not think of it this way, but date night is a habit that we cultivate for the good of our marriages. And random times of playing video games with your kids is also a life habit, which can be a good one if not done to excess. On the other hand, if you *don't* take time to do anything your kids enjoy doing, that in itself is a habit—a very poor one.

Communication skills. The habits of speaking and listening are also important ones to develop in the family sphere. When your spouse says he or she wants to tell you something, what you do next shows what habits you've developed, for better or worse. The habit of communication is extremely important in family relationships because your communication is indicative of your heart (Matt. 12:34), and your listening skills are actually a matter of obedience to God (James 1:19). In addition to speaking and listening, other communication habits include transparency, asking questions, volunteering information to keep the conversation going, and the basic but important habit of simply *responding*. If you often don't respond to text or voice messages, that's a habit that can be very destructive to relationships.

Family Meals. Eating together is a habit that creates a space for you to spend regular time with your family. There's nothing magical about sitting at a table and eating in the presence of each other, of course, but it's what the practice promotes—common interests, communication, honoring each other, and so forth. To cultivate this habit, you'll have to practice some others, like parents and older children getting home on time, inviting grandparents with enough advance notice, etc.

Resolving Conflict. Conflict resolution is as important to the members of a family as de-arming landmines is to soldiers on a battlefield. You'll need to develop habits of seeking and granting forgiveness (Eph. 4:32). You'll need to know when to say something about rude behavior and when to overlook it (1 Pet. 4:8). And you'll need to practice loving confrontation of other family members when you're not able to overlook the offense (Matt. 18:15-16).

You are already practicing habits of conflict resolution in your family—it's just a question of whether they are good ones or bad ones. Bad habits in this area of life, left unchanged, are a primary reason why divorce and other kinds of broken relationships occur in families. But there is no reason to fear estrangement when you have good habits of resolving conflict biblically.

You are already practicing habits of conflict resolution in your family—it's just a question of whether they are good ones or bad ones.

Honoring and serving each other. Consider two siblings: one is old enough to drive and the other is not. The older sibling can be the chauffer for the younger sibling as a means of honoring and serving both the sibling and the parents. However, in order for that older sibling to cultivate a good relationship, the younger sibling needs to honor the older one in some way. Perhaps gas money? Or buying dinner when they go out?

There are some family members, especially in an extended family, who can't serve much—the aging grandparent or the newborn baby, for instance. But everyone else in a family should be serving and honoring each other out of habit. We help around their house; they help around ours. We watch their kids; they watch ours. They need help moving a big piece of furniture; we need help moving a big piece of furniture. No family can thrive when there is a one-way street of honoring and serving.

VOCATIONAL SPHERE

As previously stated, habits in your vocational sphere are not as important as those in your spiritual, personal, and family spheres but are more important than those in your social sphere. Their importance doesn't come from the desire to get rich or gather possessions for ourselves, however. God has called you to work industriously for his glory (Col. 3:23). Your work is a means of pleasing God and demonstrating that you value him. That's why we repeatedly see warnings in the Bible about being idle: "If anyone is not willing to work, let him not eat" (2 Thess. 3:10); "Go to the ant, O sluggard, consider her ways and be wise" (Prov. 6:6). Not prioritizing diligent work leads to idleness and, consequently, prevents healthy social relationships. To put a lot of time into social relationships and have no job would be dangerously imbalanced. So, it's important to cultivate habits like the following in your vocational sphere.

Habits of organization. How do you manage tasks, projects, correspondence, your workspace, grade sheets, and invoices? All of those are organization habits and are foundational to honoring God in your work. Get organized; keep track of what is where. Make it a habit. For some of you reading this, you need to get organized because it's hurting your work performance.

Time management. Calling all perfectionists! Everything you do cannot be perfect. Sometimes the project simply needs to be as right as possible— then finished. We are all bound by time and space, and good habits of time management help us to identify how much time to dedicate toward a project, an email, a planning session, and when to move on to something else. These habits will determine whether or not you thrive in your vocation. They can unlock upward mobility. But if you cannot manage your time, even the simplest of vocational tasks will be overwhelming for you.

> ...if you cannot manage your time, even the simplest of vocational tasks will be overwhelming for you.

Professional development. Always improving is difficult, but necessary to a good career. What are the classes, books, conferences, or other forms of training that you're accessing to constantly improve your skills? I know of people who finish one course, take a short break, and then look for the next course to take so that they are growing constantly in their profession. That is a good habit, as long as it does not infringe on other spheres that have a higher priority. Some of our professions *require* professional development, but even if they don't, we should voluntarily pursue it. Whatever your situation might be, develop a habit of always improving in your vocational skillset.

Team building. There are some meetings that are important to attend simply because you build comradery with your team while there. The habit of team building is when you frequently seek to spend time with co-workers, get to know them personally, invest in their lives, and cultivate better professional relationships to build the cohesion of the team. This habit is especially important for those who are managers.

Peer evaluation. When do you humbly ask for input from your peers? In certain corporate contexts, this is a required part of your regular assessment as an employee. But it should be happening regularly even if it is not required. Let others proactively speak into your work. Humble yourself to develop this very helpful habit.

Here are some other examples of habits in your vocational sphere:

- Serving all of your customers

- Proactive planning

- Cultivating leads

- General administration

- Honest feedback from fellow workers

- Meeting etiquette

- Managing projects

Each of those habits will make you more effective in the sphere of your vocation. And it's often vocational habits—not qualifications and education—that make someone the best employee. Some people have all the qualifications possible but can't manage a project, so it's hard for the boss to keep them around. Some have all the education in the world, but if they are terribly unorganized, they'll be passed over. Your vocational habits are equally as important as your qualifications. Your qualifications may get you the job, but your vocational habits help you keep the job and advance in it.

Your vocational habits are equally as important as your qualifications.

This is great news because it opens a treasure chest of opportunities for you to grow in your vocation! Some of us are thinking that we need to go back to school, earn a master's degree, or get a certificate to succeed. But the reality is that good vocational habits can do just as much, if not more, to advance our careers. If you are an undisciplined worker who earns a master's degree, then you will be an undisciplined worker with a master's degree! Rather than focusing on credentials, work on improving some of your vocational habits and watch how that unlocks more possibilities for you. Sharpen your skills. Volunteer for extra projects. Work thirty minutes more than other employees do. Be quicker and clearer at replying to emails. Habits like that might be what your career needs more than anything else.

SOCIAL SPHERE

In this final sphere, we are focusing on relationships outside of our family and job, like friends, neighbors, and others we fellowship with in the church. We know that we need to work on our habits in this sphere when, for instance, we are feeling lonely or involved in the distressing drama of conflict in the neighborhood or church. Here are some important habits to consider in the social sphere:

Initiating communication. It's hard to cultivate a friendship with a person who never initiates a conversation. That's a habit we need to develop. Start by identifying people you'd like to befriend and initiate contact with them.

Praying for others. This should seem fairly obvious, but a simple word like "I prayed for your uncle, how's he doing?" goes a long way in relationships.

Responding to their text messages and calls. Hello! If you have a friend that only gets back to you when he or she wants something, you get disenchanted with that relationship before too long. That's because the habit of responding to communication is one that we have to develop, and some people never do.

Creating time to be with them. What do your friends like to do? How can you make time to do that with them? What one friend enjoys another friend might hate, so we first need to be clear on which friend likes which activity. Some of my friends would simply enjoy a coffee together, while others would rather watch a football game. Practice the habit of creating time to be with your friends, doing what they like to do.

Seeking ways to meet their needs. Most of us don't enjoy helping our friends work on their new house! But they are our friends, so we have developed the habit of helping them whether we like it or not. This is simply a way of proactively seeking to bless them, and there are many others. Do they need help with their stove or gutters? Do they need to borrow the car? Do they need a ride? Do their kids need a ride? Make a habit of meeting the needs of others, especially your brothers and sisters in Christ (Gal. 6:10).

Listening. As with family, our friendships are cultivated through good communication. And listening is arguably the most important habit of this area of our lives. We need to be "quick to hear, slow to speak," as James 1:19 says.

Getting to know your neighbors. This is a habit you develop. Do you pause and say hello, or do you just shut the garage door? Even one-to-two-minute conversations can go a long way toward cultivating kind relationships with your neighbors. Make it a habit to greet your neighbors when they're walking by—ask them which house they live in, what they do for a living, and so forth.

Serving at your local church. Part of the social sphere of your life is the local church to which you belong. If you're not connected to others in the church, it's going to be difficult to attend worship without feeling isolated and lonely. And one of the best ways to get connected is to develop habits of service in the church. If you do, a deeper sense of fellowship and friendship will grow with an increasing number of brothers and sisters in that spiritual family.

> *…one of the best ways to get connected is to develop habits of service in the church.*

Preferring their preferences. Personally, I don't find game nights particularly enjoyable. I think that there are some great games, but I'd rather just sit around and chat. However, when friends ask if I want to play a game, I've been cultivating the habit of saying yes because that's what they enjoy doing.

It's difficult to be friends with certain people because they don't have a habit of preferring others. It always has to be their choice where to eat, doing what they want to do during the time that they want to do it. Those relationships get a bit taxing because we will accommodate, but it's a challenge to continue if they never prefer us over themselves.

Remembering special occasions. It's important to remember special occasions in others' lives because those occasions are important to them, and they will notice if we remember or not. If your friend confides in you that he or she has a job interview or a scary doctor's appointment coming up, and you never follow up to ask about how it went, then you're on the way to developing a really bad habit. If you continue that way, you will not only disappoint your friends, but you'll find they won't tell you such things anymore.

Finally, here are a few more examples of good habits to practice in the social sphere:

- Not talking over people when they speak

- Remembering people's names after they've introduced themselves

- Recalling personal details about a person and using those to help facilitate conversation

- Having a right understanding of a person and their role as it relates to you

- Pausing to say hello, rather than continuing to walk by

- Not looking at your phone while in conversation

Obviously there is some overlap between the social sphere and other spheres in your life—for example, practicing the kinds of habits we've just talked about are also important in your family and vocational spheres. So, as you work through the spheres to identify which habits to work on first, you might realize at this point that some of these social habits are more important than others because they are affecting other more important spheres of life. Those who are bad listeners with their  friends or fellow church members, for instance, are often bad listeners at home and work too. So it might be a conversation with a friend that helps you see what you also need to work on in the other spheres of your life.

CHAPTER 11

A CASE STUDY FOR PRIORITIZING HABIT DEVELOPMENT

Steps of Habit Development:
Prioritizing Habits

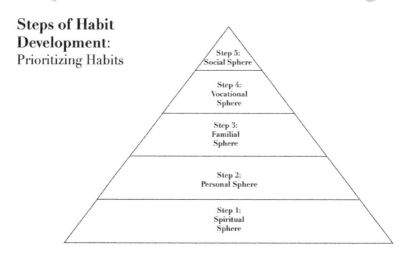

FIGURE 9: Prioritizing Habits

The figure above is another way to remember the priorities of habits in the different spheres of life (see Chapter 9). It also illustrates how the spiritual sphere is foundational to the rest of the spheres, the personal sphere is foundational to the ones above it, and so forth. The numbered "steps" indicate where we should start and how we should proceed through the different spheres of life in our habit development.

CONCURRENT PRIORITIZATION

Sometimes there will be a habit in Step 4 or 5 that needs to be developed with urgency, but you realize that there are some more fundamental habits that also need to develop before you focus on them. You will need to prioritize both concurrently. That means yes, you should focus on the vocational habit that must change now. But you also should focus on developing the habit of reading your Bible, for instance, if you have been neglecting that. This is one reason that I suggest choosing a multiple number of habits to work on at one time, rather than just one. If you chose to use your Sunday mornings to organize your work email, rather than go to church, that would be an example of overly prioritizing an urgent habit. So, that's why you should concurrently prioritize habits in the spiritual and personal spheres when you work on an urgent one in the less important ones.

Problems will often lead to urgent prioritization—and that's entirely legitimate! If your boss has reprimanded you for losing paperwork for an important bid, then you do need to work on your habit of organization. However, you cannot let problems lead you to work on only one habit or you will likely create more problems for yourself. Concurrent prioritization means that this problem for which you've been reprimanded at work is significant, but you also need to create or improve habits like being in the Bible regularly, attending church, sleeping enough, and spending time with family. If we're not sleeping well or we're spending too much time on hobbies, for example, then we would need to concurrently prioritize new habits in the personal sphere as we work on our habit of organization.

Think a little more about how the tyranny of the urgent can cause other problems for you. Imagine this scenario: your boss reprimands you, so you go into hyper-drive to develop better habits of organization. Now you become much more organized, but to do that you've started working an additional two hours per day while missing important family events and neglecting various aspects of personal health. You *are more organized* than you were before you were reprimanded, but because you allowed the problem to dictate your

For Christians especially, there are more important things in life than our vocation.

focus, you actually are worse off. For Christians especially, there are more important things in life than our vocation.

A CASE STUDY

To help you prepare for your own Personal Growth Worksheet when we get to Chapter 13, and to assist you in learning how to counsel others, let's consider the story of Brian and assess the habits he should develop and the priorities he should have.

Brian is a 40-year-old man who is married to Ashley and has three children. He and his wife rarely make it to church and often spend the weekends taxiing kids to sporting events all throughout their region. Brian feels as if they are living on the  brink of financial disaster because much of their travel expenses are being put on the credit card with hopes of paying it off when the sports season slows down. Because of his "all-in" attitude toward their kids' sports, Brian doesn't have any significant social relationships. He has a few guys that he'll talk to at work, but nothing where they will go spend time together outside of work. Brian always seems to be too busy to spend time with other friends.

Brian is feeling the effects of his choices now more than ever. He's seeing his kids care more about sports than about God and his marriage is child-centered—he and Ashley have very little time together apart from the kids. Recently, he and Ashley were on the sidelines at another game and he realized that their conversations were almost entirely about their kids. They have seemingly little in common outside of that. When club sports are not going on, Brian really doesn't have much else to do or anyone with whom to spend time. He feels lonely and Ashley has even started encouraging him to find some good friends and get out of the house a bit more.

Using the list below, identify some habits that Brian should work on in each sphere of life:

1. **Spiritual:** _____

2. **Personal:** _____

3. **Familial:** _____

4. **Vocational:** _____

5. **Social:** _____

If the first thing you thought of was that Brian needs to do is go spend time with some male friends, then you have missed the point of Chapter 9 and the beginning of this one. Re-read those as soon as possible! But if you thought that the first thing Brian needs to do is begin to attend church regularly (spiritual sphere), then you would be on the right track. Brian has prioritized family over God and needs to re-prioritize God over family by making a habit of regularly attending a local church. His kids' apathy toward God is almost certainly related to their lack of involvement in a Christian community.

The personal sphere comes next. Brian is living on the brink of financial disaster because of his use of credit cards—this is a personal habit. He and Ashley have to develop new financial habits, like living on a budget. Sooner or later, poor habits in this area will catch up to them, and though it may seem loving to invest so much in the kids now, endangering the family with poor financial decisions will not be good for them in the long term.

From the story, it seems that some of Brian's family habits are good, but not his time with Ashley. They need time alone, too. Brian has invested a lot in his kids, but he hasn't invested as much in his relationship with his wife—that's an inversion of biblical priorities. Perhaps a habit that Brian needs to work on in the family sphere is date nights with Ashley—or "date breakfasts," where they wake up early to eat together or go on a walk, just the two of them. Whatever they decide to do, Brian needs to develop the habit of time alone with his wife.

Finally, we don't know much about Brian's vocational sphere, but we do know something about his social sphere—he has very few social relationships. He's often "too busy" to spend time with potential friends and is now feeling the effects of that busyness. Brian needs to develop habits of communication with friends, habits of spending time with friends, and habits of serving friends. He doesn't seem to care about social relationships until he has none, and then feels lonely. Well, it's not a big mystery how that happened—if you stop investing in social relationships in a habitual way, you lose them. That's what Brian has done.

With all that in mind, here's what a habit development plan for Brian might look like (in order of priority):

1. **Spiritual:** Attend church weekly, disciple kids

2. **Personal:** Financial budgeting

3. **Familial:** Date nights with Ashley

4. **Vocational:** N/A

5. **Social:** Communication, time together, and investing in friends

Because of the foundational importance of our thought habits, the following goal could also be added to either the spiritual, personal, or social spheres: Every time Brian feels lonely, he will choose to pray specifically for someone else and think about a way he could serve that person.

This case study illustrates why it is helpful to understand the spheres of life when it comes to habit development. Brian's life doesn't seem like a total train wreck at this point, and there is no "hair-on-fire" moment that has forced him to pause life and get things together. However, some of his habits in the spiritual, personal, and family spheres will likely lead to disaster if he doesn't address them. If we said to him, "Hey Brian, you need to go to poker night with your buddies every two weeks," and that's all we said, we've missed some of the more significant habits Brian needs to develop, like attending church and cultivating his personal relationship with Jesus. After all, how can we expect to develop Christian community if we are not attending church?

In the end, the spheres of life are just a way of conceptualizing the priorities that God has given to us. That's why we start with the spiritual habits and then progress outward to the other spheres, because we want to glorify God and do good to others in our habit development. Now you're ready to go more in-depth in evaluating the habits in your own life, and helping others to do so. That's what the next chapter is about.

CHAPTER 12

TAKING
INVENTORY

"All change is preceded by knowledge." Hmm. What does that mean? As you look at your life, you might see what I called "presentation problems" (Chapter 5)—habits that are problematic but might not be the source cause. You may not easily be able to see what underlying issues you need to work on in order to solve the problem. That's because of a lack of knowledge. You cannot change if you are unaware of what needs to change. This is the meaning of "all change is preceded by knowledge."

This chapter will be different from the others, because most of it will be an inventory questionnaire. It is designed to help you learn about *you* (or perhaps give to others you are trying to help). Its purpose is to help you grow in knowledge about yourself and your habits—the ones you already have and the ones you might need to develop. The questions are grouped into four categories: sinful habits, unhelpful habits, sanctifying habits, and helpful habits. The categories are listed in order of importance, and the questions within each category are listed according to the priority of the spheres of life. Here is an explanation of each category (the first two are bad habits and the second two are good ones):

A sinful habit is something you frequently and regularly practice that is clear disobedience to a command in the Word of God. You might speak in a way that is harsh and harmful to others, for instance, and that habit of communication grieves the Holy Spirit (Eph. 4:29-30). Sinful habits are the first areas in your life that you need to change. The Bible makes it clear that for you to grow, you must start by putting off sinful thoughts and actions (Eph. 4:22; Col. 3:9). So, our inventory will start there.

Unhelpful habits are habits that are not inherently sinful, but are not wise and profitable for our lives. You could practice these habits and have no spiritual barrier between you and God. An example of this kind of habit would be not maintaining a calendar, or other forms of poor time management. Failing to maintain a calendar doesn't necessarily mean that you are in sin, but it does mean that you will probably not be as efficient and productive as you could be.

Sanctifying habits are habits that are directly encouraged in the Bible as ways of glorifying God. They are often the opposite of sinful habits. The Bible says that in order to change, we must not only "put off" certain actions, but we must "put on" others to replace them (Eph. 4:24; Col. 3:12). Sanctifying habits are those we must "put on." To use an example from above, if you have a habit of speaking harshly and harmfully, then you should replace that with a habit of using pleasant words (Prov. 16:29), or words that build up others (Eph. 4:29). Some of the most important sanctifying habits are those that are often called "the means of grace"—learning the Word, prayer, service, fellowship, and observing baptism and the Lord's Supper.

...we must not only "put off" certain actions, but we must "put on" others to replace them...

The final category in the inventory is helpful habits. These habits are not mentioned in the Bible as inherently sanctifying but can make it easier for us to achieve the goals we have for our daily lives. They include things like organizing your schedule, writing down people's names, spending time with friends, returning phone calls, and so forth. Like in the category of unhelpful habits, problems in this category are not necessarily sinful. For instance, it isn't necessarily a sin to be in the habit of not returning your friends' phone calls. But it sure would make for a stronger relationship if you did, and that can lead to further spiritual profit.

A few final comments before we get to the inventory: First, these questions are not exhaustive or comprehensive. This is a primer to help you get started and identify some areas to grow and change. Second, I suggest that as you go through the list for the first time, simply circle the questions that apply to you the most, or list the bad habits you want to stop and the good ones you want to develop based on the questions. Don't write down how you will go about changing at this point. Later, I will provide a worksheet that you can utilize for that purpose.

INVENTORY OF HABITS

Sinful Habits

Spiritual

+ Do you have thoughts about God that are blasphemous or disrespectful?
+ Do you skip church regularly?
+ Do you not give sacrificially to your local church?
+ Do you not read your Bible?
+ Do you avoid using your gifts in serving others?
+ Do you meditate on untruths rather than the truths of God's Word?
+ Do you take repentance seriously?
+ Do you pray regularly?

Personal

+ Do you think about yourself in ways that are contrary to what God has said?
+ Do you use your body for pure purposes—in what you view, in how you relate to others, and in what you say?
+ Do you exercise discipline of yourself in a daily capacity?
+ Do you manage your time according to God's priorities?
+ Do you eat proper amounts of food?
+ Does your exercise routine reflect biblical principles of stewardship?
+ Do your personal finances represent biblical principles of stewardship?

Familial

+ Do you allow negative and spiteful thoughts about family members to fester in your mind?
+ Do you prioritize time with your kids, your spouse, your parents?
+ Do you seek to honor your family in ways appropriate to your relationship with them?
+ Do you prioritize your family over your work by keeping clear boundaries to protect your family?
+ Do you make decisions that prioritize your family?
+ Is unity with your spouse your first priority outside of God in your life?
+ Are you discipling your kids in the Bible?
+ Are you taking your kids to church or other children's and youth ministries?

Vocational

+ Do you frequently rue your job in your mind, rather than being thankful for it?
+ Do you view your job as only a way to make money, rather than serving God and others?
+ Do you work honestly without supervision?
+ Do you admit your mistakes at work?
+ Do you work hard to earn a sufficient amount of income?
+ Do you stay on task and follow a task through until its completion?

Social

+ Do you have Christian social relationships?
+ Do you think that you don't need them in your life?
+ Do you resolve conflict according to the Bible?
+ Do you communicate in relationships according to the Bible?
+ Do you serve other people with the gifts God has given you?
+ Do you allow unbiblical social relationships to be your dating relationships?
+ Do you forgive, as the Lord as forgiven you?

Unhelpful Habits

Spiritual

- Do you often move between churches?
- Do you allow hobbies to be scheduled during church times?
- Do you watch TV more than you read your Bible?
- Do you irregularly give to your local church?
- Do you not serve others on a regular basis?
- Do you spend too much time thinking about earthly things and not enough about heavenly ones?

Personal

- Do you think more about the way you appear to others, or what God thinks about you?
- Do you use your phone too much—frittering away your time, watching unimportant media, etc.?
- Do you often run on little sleep?
- Do you often eat very poorly (nutritionally)?
- Do you start exercising, only to quit within a few weeks?
- Do you use a calendar to manage your time?
- Do you fail to follow through on a personal budget?

Family

- Do you fill your mind with entertainment that may cause you to think negatively about your family?
- Do you limit your bills so you are not required to work too much?
- Do you regularly neglect family time?
- Do your hobbies regularly take time from your spouse without his or her permission?
- Do you not disciple your kids in the Bible?
- Do your kids' teachers spend more time with your kids than you do?

Vocational

- Do you ever pray for your boss or co-workers?
- Do you show up to work late regularly?
- Do you not manage your own tasks without being told?
- Do you learn very slowly?
- Do you express your opinions too often about decisions at work?
- Are you disagreeable at work?
- Do you regularly seek to improve your work performance?

Sanctifying Habits

Spiritual

- Do you regularly attend a local church?
- Do you regularly read the Bible?
- Are you meditating on the Bible throughout your day?
- Are you involved in fellowship at a local church?
- Are you serving others with the gifts God has given you?
- Are you faithfully and sacrificially giving to your church?
- Do you "pray without ceasing"?

Personal

- Do you accept how God has made you and thank him for it?
- Are you being a good steward of your money?
- Are you disciplining yourself to eat proper amounts of food?
- Do you limit your work and hobbies to get enough sleep?
- Do you use your time in ways that would honor the Lord?
- Are you being pure with your body?
- Is the hobby you maintain something that honors the Lord?

Family

- Do you pray for your family members regularly?
- Do you make family time a priority?
- Do have a regular time with just your spouse?

+ Do you spend time studying the Bible with your family?
+ Do you attend church together as a family?
+ Do you prioritize significant family events over work (e.g., birthdays, weddings, etc.)?
+ Do you spend meaningful time with each of your kids?

Vocational

+ Do you work hard while you're at work?
+ Do you come to work on time?
+ Do you think of your job as a way to worship and serve God?
+ Do you fulfill your tasks that are assigned by your boss?
+ Do you communicate well with employees, employers, and customers?
+ Are you a worker whom others can depend on?
+ Are you a worker whom is competent in your job due to hard work and growing in skills?

Helpful Habits

Spiritual

+ Do you take notes while at church?
+ Do you go to bed on time to be ready for church the next morning?
+ Do you serve regularly in your church?
+ Are you committed to a plan for reading the Bible?
+ Do you have any goals in mind for how you'd like to grow this year?
+ Is there a group of people that you can reach out to if you're in need?

Personal

+ Do you manage your time?
+ Do you have a calendar?
+ Do you have budgetary goals?
+ Do you know what a balanced meal should entail?
+ Do you get enough sleep to ensure you are well rested?
+ Do you refuse to waste time?
+ Do you work toward goals yearly?
+ Do you set goals for yourself?

Family

+ Do you communicate regularly with family members?
+ Do you remember special holidays?
+ Do you initiate time with family?
+ Do you work regularly to bless individual members of your family?
+ Do you play with your kids?
+ Do you walk with your spouse?
+ Do you call before going home?
+ Do you go home when you've committed to going home?
+ Do you tuck your kids into bed?

Vocational

+ Do you respond to emails?
+ Do you return phone calls?
+ Do you manage a professional calendar?
+ Do you plan for professional projects?
+ Do you regularly improve your skillset by additional training?
+ Do you seek input into your work performance?

Social

+ Do you seek out conversation with new people?
+ Are you available to spend time with?
+ Do you prioritize others' schedules and make yourself available to them?
+ Do you work on your communication with others?
+ Do you actively listen?
+ Do you remember names of people that you've met?
+ Do you maintain accurate expectations of your friends?
+ Do you include friends into the personal details of your life?
+ Do you share information about yourself?
+ Do you do small talk with friends to cultivate common interests?

CHAPTER 13

APPLYING THE TRUTH ABOUT HABITS

As I am writing this, there are no other Christian books focused solely on habit development. I'm sure that will eventually change, but right now you don't have a lot of options if you're looking for help with working on your habits. So, in conclusion, I want to give you a few ideas about how to use this book, which hopefully will make it more helpful and effective for you going forward.

PRACTICAL STEPS

To start, always seek more understanding of your heart as it pertains to your life. What is taking place at the level of your heart? Are you motivated by pleasing God? Do you want to glorify him? Remember that the primary goals of your habits should be to glorify God and do good to others. Be sure those motivations propel you into faithful habit development.

Second, always remember the relative priorities of the spheres of life. In so doing, you will keep before you the ultimate importance of your relationship with God and cultivating spiritual habits. You should grow in excellence and correct problematic habits, but do so in order of biblical priority. Be careful not to allow anything of lesser importance overshadow something that matters more to God and others.

Third, identify key habits that you need to develop. Perhaps consider areas of weakness? What regular thoughts or actions can you simply not allow to continue? Take what you've learned in this book and let it become an impetus for you to grow in those areas. You have the resources—now it's time to implement what you know.

Finally, set a regular, periodic time to evaluate habits in your life. New Year's is a very natural time for this—you can sit down in December/January and make some goals for what you want to accomplish in the coming year. Having a regular time for evaluation can prevent you from waiting until things get dire before you make changes. Every year or more frequently, you could also go to a counselor, a professional coach, a financial coach, a nutritionist, a fitness trainer, or other advisors. There are many resources to help you grow—take advantage of these regularly. Don't wait until the potential problem becomes a problem. Good maintenance helps things operate smoothly.

A FINAL ENCOURAGEMENT

As you're finishing this book, the only shame would be for you to not do anything! Change isn't magical—it's degree is often correspondent to the level of effort that you invest in the process. Rather than starting with grandiose plans that aren't likely to happen, pick two or three habits that you'd like to grow in and do it! Change doesn't take place in the abstract: change takes place in concrete, down-in-the-weeds-of-life  ways. Pick two or three specific ways to implement this book and grow in those areas! It's better to try and fail than not to try at all! Remember, faithfulness is what we're aiming for—it's not perfection, but *direction* that God expects from us. Jesus died for all the ways we fail and he loves us anyway. So get started in the direction of some new habits for the glory of God and the good of others!

What changes do you want to make? Use this worksheet to work through your plan for them…

HEART & HABITS: PERSONAL GROWTH WORKSHEET

Habit

The habit that I want to develop is …

Example: "Managing my time while at work by spending 15 minutes each day on my extra project in order to complete projects ahead of schedule."

_____

_____

_____

_____

_____

_____

Heart

My first goal is to please God by …

Example: "I want to please God by developing a better habit of time management and being more structured with my time."

_____

_____

_____

_____

Secondarily, my habit will do good to people by ...

> Example: "My habit will benefit my boss and customers by me
> completing tasks according to schedule."

_____

_____

_____

_____

_____

Sphere of Life

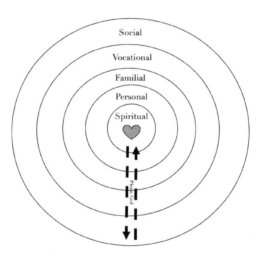

The habit I'm working on corresponds to the _____ sphere of life. (Write down the sphere for each habit you are working on.)

Steps of Habits

Steps of Habit Development:
Prioritizing Habits

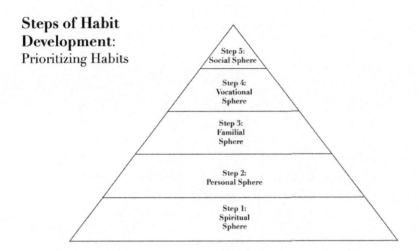

I realize that there may be some more foundational habits that I must also work on from the **Steps of Habits.** Here are one or two more habits from spheres that are below my chosen one on the "priority pyramid":

Examples: "Spiritual Sphere: More regular church attendance"
and "Vocational Sphere: Managing my work
calendar more accurately."

+ _____ Sphere:

_____

+ _____ Sphere:

_____

+ _____ Sphere:

_____

Frequency of Habits

Example: "My goal for frequency in practicing
this habit is five times per week."

My goal for frequency in practicing this habit is _____ times per _____.

Community

Example: "I will ask my friend _____ to encourage
me and register with me for a class on learning
better time-management habits."

_____
_____
_____
_____
_____

Environment

Example: "I'm going to cancel my television cable for 90 days
to help me develop the habit of time management."

_____
_____
_____
_____
_____

Finally, I will log my success in sticking to the frequency of the habit that I'm attempting to develop. This can be in a journal, checklist paper, app for my smart phone, or any other means. The log will look something like this:

Habit	Manage my time better by working 15 minutes each day toward this project.						
Day	**Mon**	**Tue**	**Wed**	**Thu**	**Fri**	**Sat**	**Sun**
Complete?	Y/N	Y/N	Y/N	Y/N	Y/N	Y/N	Y/N

He who is the blessed and only Sovereign, the King of kings and Lord of lords, who alone has immortality, who dwells in unapproachable light, whom no one has ever seen or can see. To him be honor and eternal dominion. Amen.

— 1 Timothy 6:15-16

MORE EDUCATION OR NEW HABITS?

An interesting question has arisen in my many discussions with students and other faculty in my role as a college professor:

What is more beneficial about higher education—learning a body of knowledge or developing habits of discipline, timeliness, project management, communication, sustained focus, and so forth? Are you paying primarily for a body of knowledge or for a skillset? Well, let's think through what you may remember (or not) from Philosophy 101: who is René Descartes and what was he famous for? Go on…. Who is he…. What was he famous for? Uh huh…

Hopefully your philosophy course had some important content, but it was equally as valuable (at least) for you to learn how to listen to the professor and ask questions (a vocational habit), how to use a calendar (a personal habit), how to study for a test (personal/vocational), how to maintain your devotions while taking classes (spiritual), and how to maintain family/friend relationships while you took classes (social). College teaches you more than a body of knowledge—it teaches you habits that will last the rest of your life.

But every time you're on the internet, you'll see or hear another advertisement from a college enticing you to go back to school, enroll in their degree program, and "advance yourself." Is it possible that college is indeed valuable, but not for the reasons usually given? Earning your Master's degree might unlock a credential for you, sure. But it's not only the credential that's of value to you. It's the habits that you learn while pursuing that credential.

Maybe we don't need more education per se, but we need the good habits that pursuing more education brings for us?

Here are a handful of habits that pursuing more education helps us to develop:

+ **Spiritual Sphere**: Learning to prioritize habits like Bible reading, church attendance, and Bible studies while balancing homework and classes.

+ **Personal Sphere**: Maintaining sleep, proper nutrition, learning how to pay for your school while living on a budget, and time management via assignment due dates.

+ **Family Sphere**: Family time outside of school, investing in family relationships while busy, and prioritizing family over school.

+ **Vocational Sphere**: Listening to your boss's intent, understanding priorities of projects, time management, working with colleagues, receiving critical feedback, balancing multiple tasks, and learning to ask questions.

+ **Social Sphere**: Prioritizing time together with friends while in school, communication skills with friends, and honoring and serving friends while in school.

When a professor says, "Oral Presentation on René Descartes due Friday," you have to kick into gear spiritual habits, personal habits, family habits, vocational habits, and social habits. You also have a community of people that are holding you accountable to these habits—your class and professor. From answering the question "What grade did you get?" to having the professor grade you, it's all a communal effort. And one of the best ways to develop habits is in community, as we said in Chapter 6. So, when you successfully complete an assignment and get a passing grade, you also have successfully managed habits that enabled you to get a good grade on that assignment. Your class and professor are a great means of helping you cultivate new habits.

But you also have a vested interest because of your tuition payments. You have a bill that you or your parents are paying, and you feel as if you're wasting money if you don't follow through with coursework (which you *are*, to be sure!). However, with a vested financial interest in your schooling, you have incentivized the development of habits. Or, to put it another way, you've de-incentivized the failure of coursework. In habit formation, some would consider this as the reward component to your habit development: your reward is not wasting money!

Next, there is the time factor—remember that we said that faithfulness is the goal, as opposed to frequency? Pursuing a degree requires faithfulness. Most degree programs are comprised of semesters and most semesters are at least 6-8 weeks. This means you cannot just be disciplined for one week-end—it must be sustained for more than a short period, and before long, it just feels like the right thing to do. Many graduates, upon no longer having homework, still have a compulsion to study. That's because they've developed a personal habit of study. And their calendar is accustomed to having times of study to fill it! When a student graduates, they've spent years studying and no longer have to study. Something doesn't feel right. The semester structure of attending college helps you to develop habits because you're practicing them for several months at a time.

So, do you need more education or do you need new habits? The answer is that you really do need new habits, but those habits might best come through more education. By the time you're done with that new degree, certificate, or credential, you will have developed new habits. And it's the course of study that has helped you to develop the habits. Nothing against René Descartes, but we need the habits that college brings just as much as we need the body of knowledge that college delivers.

Thus, instead of thinking, *What's the quickest way to earn a degree?* you should see the process as part of the product. If you could write a $50,000 check to an institution of higher education and receive a degree from them without any classwork, you should decline that option because you need the process, too, not just the degree. Education isn't about acquisition only. It's about becoming. Educational processes aren't just dumping information into "thought receptacles," they're forming habits in people that will last them a lifetime. Let's enjoy the process, then. Let's move without unnecessary delay through our degree programs, but also put in enough time for the process to be valuable as well.

Some people will never have the resources to go back to school: time, money, or opportunity. In that case, they should focus on the habits that schooling brings, as opposed to the credential of a degree program. This book might be a starting point for that kind of growth (an inexpensive starting point at that!). Use this book as a curriculum to help you develop good habits. But also recognize that you may need some of the additional structure that school provides: community, financial involvement, rewards, penalties, and so forth. Consider hiring a professional coach to help duplicate some of the structure of education. A coach, especially a Christian coach, can provide such structure and accountability over the long-term. If you really do mean business, then I encourage you to pursue habits of education through other creative means.

For most of us, education isn't outside of the realm of possibility—with federal aid, low interest rates, and online schooling, further education is attainable. Maybe you should go back to school this year simply for the sake of challenging yourself? Earning a degree may do absolutely nothing for your vocation, but it can do many things for your habit development. *That's worth it.*

SPHERES OF HABITS

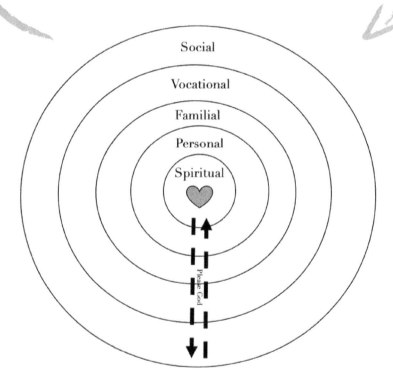

STEPS OF PRIORITIZING HABITS

Steps of Habit Development:
Prioritizing Habits

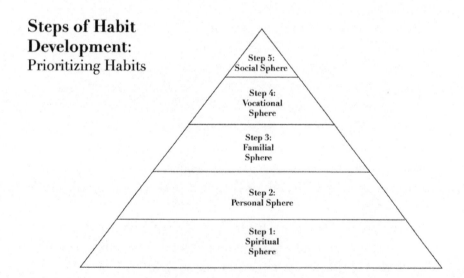

Step 5:
Social Sphere

Step 4:
Vocational
Sphere

Step 3:
Familial
Sphere

Step 2:
Personal Sphere

Step 1:
Spiritual
Sphere

ACKNOWLEDGEMENTS

I really wanted James Parker to be the co-author of this book. His multiple conversations over coffee, lunches, and phone calls made this book what it is. I'm forever indebted to your input, James. Thank you, brother.

Julie Devore was a student of mine at The Master's University who helped read, research, and re-develop the book from its beginning stages. I am immensely thankful for you, Julie, and your positive and insightful help in this project.

Stephanie Beals was a reader early on and provided me a great amount of feedback, challenging me to explain things in a more biblically articulate capacity. Frankly, Stephanie, your help created two or three chapters of new content. Thank you.

The Master's University is my home. The students at Master's are my people. I'm thankful for the opportunity to teach the future church at TMU and for the opportunity to learn alongside you.

Dave Swavely, my editor, has been a delight. You provide helpful criticisms and compliments. Thanks for "getting it" and helping to make the book a better product.

Not enough can be said for Faith Community Church, my local church. You are my family. You are my community. What a joy to be a part of your family! Thanks for loving me and my family so well.

Brian Mesimer, a new friend, and reader of this project. You're probably the most informed on the topic within the biblical counseling field, so it did the project much good to have your feedback, Brian. Thank you.

HEART
&
HABITS

Printed in Great Britain
by Amazon

87348280R00088